At Issue

| Trial by Internet

Other Books in the At Issue Series

At Issue

| Trial by Internet

Avery Elizabeth Hurt, Book Editor

GREENHAVEN
PUBLISHING

Published in 2018 by Greenhaven Publishing, LLC
353 3rd Avenue, Suite 255, New York, NY 10010

Articles in Greenhaven Publishing anthologies are often edited for length to meet page
requirements. In addition, original titles of these works are changed to clearly present
the main thesis and to explicitly indicate the author's opinion. Every effort is made to
ensure that Greenhaven Publishing accurately reflects the original intent of the authors.
Every effort has been made to trace the owners of the copyrighted material.

Cover image: enzozo/Shutterstock.com

Library of Congress Cataloging-in-Publication Data

Names: Hurt, Avery Elizabeth, editor.
Title: Trial by internet / edited by Avery Elizabeth Hurt.
Description: New York : Greenhaven Publishing, 2018. | Series: At issue | Includes
  bibliographical references and index. | Audience: Grades 9-12.
Identifiers: LCCN ISBN 9781534500693 (library bound) | ISBN 9781534500679
  (pbk.)
Subjects: LCSH: Internet--Political aspects--Juvenile literature. | Social media--
  Political aspects.
Classification: LCC HM851.T753 2018 | DDC 302.231--dc23

Manufactured in the United States of America

Website: http://greenhavenpublishing.com

Contents

Introduction

The sixth amendment of the Constitution of the United States reads simply:

In all criminal prosecutions, the accused shall enjoy the right to a speedy and public trial, by an impartial jury of the State and district wherein the crime shall have been committed, which district shall have been previously ascertained by law, and to be informed of the nature and cause of the accusation; to be confronted with the witnesses against him; to have compulsory process for obtaining witnesses in his favor, and to have the Assistance of Counsel for his defence.

Sometimes, that simple assurance of rights can be difficult to guarantee. When a person is accused of a crime—particularly a crime committed in a small town or one that is particularly newsworthy (say the murder of a well-known person, involving harm to a child, or a particularly gruesome murder)—finding an *impartial* jury can be next to impossible. Often a judge will move a trial to a town where the case is less well known so that a jury can be pulled from a group of people who do not already have an opinion about the guilt or innocence of the accused. Sometimes juries are sequestered, meaning they are kept isolated (in a hotel, for example) from contact with other people and any news that might influence their judgment. But in today's hyper-connected world, keeping a jury from being influenced by the press and the public can be extremely difficult. Like everyone else, jurors have smart phones and social media accounts. They are exposed not only to news reports about the case they are hearing, but to the opinions and input of pretty much anyone who decides to hold forth about the case on Twitter or Facebook. In cases with high emotional interest, it can be very difficult for defendants to get fair trials.

Nonetheless, most jurors do take the responsibilities of jury duty seriously and make every effort to limit their judgment to the facts presented in court and to abide by the instructions of the judge. The jurors in the case of O. J. Simpson, who was charged with murdering his wife and a male friend, and those who heard the case of Casey Anthony—charged with the murder of her young daughter—rendered verdicts consistent with the evidence, at the risk of a great deal of censure from a public that was firmly convinced of the guilt of the defendants. It was even at the expense of the evidence, in the case of Anthony, and the rules of evidence, in the case of Simpson.

Even when defendants are found not guilty in court, the fallout from being declared guilty in the court of public opinion can last for years. Of course, this is not new in the Internet Age—or even before it! The phrase "trial by media" has been around longer than the World Wide Web and refers to television or newspaper coverage that creates the perception of guilt or innocence before, during, or after a criminal trial. In 1954, Sam Sheppard, a physician in Cleveland, Ohio, was accused of the brutal murder of his pregnant wife, Marilyn. He was convicted amidst a media circus and newspaper headlines that had assumed his guilt before he was even arrested. In 1966, in *Sheppard v. Maxwell, Warden*, the Supreme Court ruled that prejudicial pretrial publicity had prevented Sheppard from getting a fair trial and ordered that he be released from prison. He was retried and acquitted in the second trial.

It is important for the media to cover court cases and make sure the rights of defendants are upheld and respected by the courts. However, the media is also responsible for presenting accurate information and respecting the court's decisions about what can and cannot be made public. Journalists know this; they may not always act responsibly, but they are held to professional standards by their employers as well as the ethics of their profession. Individuals on social media are under no such restrictions. There is no law against gossip, and increasingly little social taboo against it. Social media can easily and quickly turn from citizens speaking truth to power and holding the judicial system accountable for its practices to a virtual lynch mob.

However, it is not just criminal cases where so-called "trial by internet" can result in a miscarriage of justice. Gossip is nothing new, but social media has made it possible for gossip to spread quickly and have a worldwide reach. In this text you will read about people being accused of child abuse and sexual assault—with no evidence other than the claims of the accusers—then "tried and convicted" on social media. People lose jobs, families, and standing in their communities, all based on what is essentially a very powerful form of gossip. Attempts to convict Amanda Knox in the court of public opinion became something of a cottage industry.

It is not only people who have been accused of a crime who are victims of trial by internet. Reputations have been damaged—often beyond repair— by accusations of professional impropriety, and often just plain slander and bullying. Despite its very obvious virtues, the internet can be a dangerous weapon.

Evaluating a person—or a person's guilt or innocence—via the internet is obviously fraught. But in a more subtle and in a potentially even more dangerous way, trial by internet can be applied to our national conversation. Lies, false news, and other poorly sourced and unattributed information, when widely circulated, can interfere with the smooth operation of democracy. No matter what one's political leanings or policy preferences, in order to make sound decisions about national policy and political candidates, one needs accurate information. Unfortunately, on the internet, it can be difficult to determine accuracy.

The following viewpoints address the many ways trial by internet can cause problems for individuals and society at large. A few offer possible solutions, or at least ideas for mitigating the damage done by trial by internet in its various forms. But in the end, the only real solution is for people to take responsibility for what they write and what they share and to make an effort to check the value and sources of the information they read—wherever they find it.

1

Trial by Facebook Is a Dangerous Trend

Craig Charles

Craig Charles is the founding editor of, and a primary contributor to, the website That's Nonsense. The site, established in 2009, is dedicated to debunking internet hoaxes, rumors, hearsay, and fake news.

What exactly constitutes "trial by internet"? In this article, Craig Charles uses recent examples to clearly explain what the phenomenon is. He also describes the possible ramifications for individuals who are "tried" in this way, for the people who engage in spreading unverified information, and, in the long run, for our system of justice. In addition, readers will also find advice—and a stern warning— about the dangers of spreading false information or engaging in internet vigilantism.

We've seen it a lot lately. Posts identifying "guilty" individuals imploring others to identify, condemn, even exact revenge, on the people identified.

It's called *Trial by Facebook* or *Trial by Social Media* and it involves the posting of content on Facebook or other social media that identifies and condemns individuals allegedly guilty of a crime and implores others to share the content, thus exposing the accused to an angry public.

Such content goes further than to simply lay out the facts of an incident. *Trial by Social Media/Facebook* content condemns and

"Social Media Witch Hunts—Why You Need to Avoid Them," by Craig Charles, ThatsNonsense.com, January 18, 2017. Reprinted by permission.

judges, often unfairly or without proof. And it is for that reason it is potentially dangerous and unjust. Such posts play judge, jury and executioner.

Trial by Facebook content will often explicitly condone vigilante justice, but even if it does not then it will always—to some extent—encourage it implicitly.

Resisting this type of behaviour can often prove difficult. We may feel that the people identified in the photos could arguably deserve being shamed in the public arena, and that by doing so we would discourage others from committing similar offenses.

Often *Trial by Facebook/Social Media* posts result from knee-jerk and impassioned reactions where we become the unwitting victims of our own emotions, only doing what makes us feel better in the short term rather than looking at the bigger picture.

However, we live in a world with legal justice systems, and whether you agree or disagree with your legal system or with a specific sentence handed out, there is still *never* a place in any civilised world for vigilante justice. And vigilante justice is exactly what *Trial by Facebook* promotes and encourages.

And if that isn't reason enough to stop you posting *Trial by Social Media* content, then here is a whole bunch of other reasons.

Inaccurate Content?

Trial by Social media posts can often accumulate thousands, even hundreds of thousands of shares. And sadly the vast majority of people who share this type of content will do so without any verification or proof that it is accurate.

We never condone sharing such content even if you know it to be genuine—but blindly sharing it without verifying it is both irresponsible and negligent on an entirely different level. Not to mention dangerous.

And of course this can lead to innocent people facing difficulties in their lives, even facing the possibility of physical attacks. Not to mention people passing on such false information to their friends can themselves be sued and/or prosecuted under an array of charges including libel.

An example? Ask anyone called Thierry Mairot, who likely faced a difficult time after an entirely false rumour claiming he was a sexual predator trying to seduce children on Facebook spread like wildfire, when thousands of Facebook users circulated the rumour without verification. Or perhaps ask David Calvert, who was at the tail-end of a Facebook campaign falsely identifying him as James Bulger killer, Jon Venables.

Imagine if a false rumour identified you? Would you want people to spread it? Think about that before hitting Share.

Mistaken Identity?

Regardless if a *Trial by Social Media* post contains genuine information or not, they can *still* be dangerous to innocent individuals because of mistaken identity.

Viral posts containing names can lead to innocent people with the same name being abused and attacked.

Viral posts containing photos can lead to innocent people sharing similar physical characteristics being abused or attacked.

An example? Ask anyone who shares the same name as almost any modern-day high-profile murderer, when social media rumours are blindly passed from user to user incorrectly identifying Facebook accounts as the accounts belonging to the guilty. Ask James Holmes, who received constant abuse from Facebook users convinced—after seeing a Facebook rumour condemning his profile—that he was the Aurora movie theater killer.

Legal Influences

Particularly viral posts about real cases have the potential to influence legal proceedings. So if charges are ever bought against guilty parties, damaging and libelous posts can make it difficult to prosecute. In high profile cases, *Trial by Social Media* could cause prejudice in jury pools which could potentially cause cases to be dismissed because of unfair trials.

Remember...

Remember that when you post to social media, you are publishing real content that can have real ramifications for real people. You are responsible for what you write and you are accountable for the consequences that may occur, whether they may be moral, legal, or both.

Both *Trial by Social Media* and the vigilante justice it encourages are both simply unacceptable in any civilised country. We don't live in a world where anyone gets to decide what punishment to enact because that simply cannot work. Like it or not, we abide by the laws of the country in which we reside and we accept the punitive actions given by their courts. And if you encourage or enact vigilantism then you're just as bad as anyone else who thinks crime is acceptable.

2

Forget the Electric Chair—the Internet's the Hot Seat!

Douglas Preston

Douglas Preston is a novelist and journalist who writes techno-thrillers and horror, much of it in collaboration with novelist Lincoln Child. His nonfiction book, The Monster of Florence, *about a notorious Italian serial killer, is being made into a feature film.*

In this article, Preston relates how he became swept up in the internet furor over the case of Amanda Knox, a young American woman who was accused and convicted (though that conviction was later overturned) of killing her roommate in Italy. Preston tries to determine why so many people who knew neither him nor Knox personally—who, as Preston puts it here "had no skin in the game"— were so obsessed with the case and so relentless in their hate-filled denunciations of Knox and those who dared suggest she might be innocent. Since the publication of this article, Amanda Knox was acquitted by Italy's highest court, putting an end to the case.

O n Nov. 2, 2007, in the ancient and lovely hill town of Perugia, Italy, a British girl named Meredith Kercher was found murdered in the cottage she shared with several other students. Four days later, police and prosecutors announced they had arrested the three killers, among them a 20-year-old college student from

Seattle named Amanda Knox. The ensuing investigation, trial, conviction, and appeal lasted five years. On March 26, an Italian court ruled that she must be retried for murder. The case may drag on for years to come.

One of the most disturbing aspects of this case, at least for me, was the savage outcry against Amanda on the Internet, which continues to this day. On March 29, 2013, as I was putting the final touches on this article, I conducted an experiment. I Googled "Amanda Knox" and got 7.1 million hits. I then tried "Amanda Knox" and "bitch," which returned 1.7 million hits. "Amanda Knox" and "pervert" came back at 880,000 hits, and her name coupled with "slut" yielded 380,000. The quotations that opened this article were gathered in a few minutes of surfing.

The extreme viciousness of the anti-Amanda commentariage is startling. There are countless statements calling for the murdering, raping, torturing, throat-cutting, frying, hanging, electrocution, burning, and rotting in hell of Amanda, along with her sisters, family, friends, and supporters.

Why? And why in general are there so many savage, crazy, vicious, and angry people on the Internet?

I was drawn into the case by accident. While living in Florence, I teamed up with an Italian journalist, Mario Spezi, and wrote a book about Italy's most notorious serial killer, known only as the Monster of Florence—a murderer so terrifying he makes Jack the Ripper look like Mister Rogers. Together Mario and I published a book about the case, *The Monster of Florence*. Giuliano Mignini, the chief prosecutor in the Amanda Knox case, was also the prosecutor in the Monster case. We criticized Mignini in our book. He then did to me what he would do to Amanda a year later: He hauled me in for an interrogation with no attorney or interpreter present, accused me of being an accessory to murder, among other heinous crimes, and demanded I confess. He threw Spezi into prison and accused him of being the Monster of Florence. (Later the charges against us were dropped and Mignini was investigated for abuse of office.)

I began speaking out in favor of Amanda. My first foray was in a mild interview with the journalist Candace Dempsey on the website of the *Seattle Post-Intelligencer*, the local paper in Amanda's hometown. I told of my experience with Mignini and said I thought Amanda was innocent.

Then the comments poured in. I was stunned at their ferociousness against Amanda. What surprised me also were the blazing personal attacks against me. They claimed I was exploiting a murder to sell books. They claimed that my interest in Amanda was sexual. They said I was mentally ill. They Photoshopped grotesque pictures of me and posted them. They created elaborate PowerPoint presentations that aimed to prove beyond all doubt what a contemptible, disgusting, racist, perverted, money-grubbing scumbag I truly was.

Like a fool I waded into the fray, defending Amanda and myself. I attacked my attackers and countered their criticisms. The more I fought, the more the tide of vituperation came back at me. Finally, I came to my senses and stopped. But I continued to defend Amanda on television and noticed that every time I appeared, the Internet exploded with more extreme attacks. I have no doubt that when this piece is published, the Amanda-haters will go incandescent once again. It made me wonder: Who *are* these people? Why would so many people, with no skin in the game, devote their time and energy to seeing this girl punished—and to vilifying all those who came to her defense?

I did some research. The anti-Amanda universe coalesced around three websites devoted to seeing her punished. The administrators of these sites and their followers were utterly and completely obsessed by hatred for Amanda. It had literally taken over their lives. The chief moderator of one, according to statistics on her profile, has blogged about Amanda an average of seven times per day, every day, for the past five years. The anti-Amanda writings of another add up to more words than the Bible, *War and Peace, Finnegans Wake, The Iliad,* and *The Odyssey* combined. Five years later, these websites are spewing more than ever.

The answer to this human behavior lies, as many such answers do, in evolutionary biology. Experiments show that when some people punish others, the reward part of their brain lights up like a Christmas tree. It turns out we humans avidly engage in something anthropologists call "altruistic punishment." What is altruistic punishment? It is when a person punishes someone who has done nothing against them personally but has violated what they perceive to be the norms of society. Why "altruistic"? Because the punisher is doing something that benefits society at large, with no immediate personal gain. Altruistic punishment is normally a good thing. Our entire criminal justice system is based on it. In our evolutionary past, small groups of hunter-gatherers needed enforcers, individuals who took it upon themselves to punish slackers and transgressors to maintain group cohesion. We evolved this way. As a result, some people are born to be punishers. They are hard-wired for it.

What does all this have to do with Amanda Knox? Almost all the nasty comments about her follow a pattern. Even though she did nothing to them, they are all *demanding her punishment*. This is altruistic punishment gone haywire, in which the anti-Amanda bloggers have become a cybermob not unlike the witch-hunts of medieval Europe or lynch mobs in the American South. These mobs form all over the Internet, and not just in the Amanda case, assailing everyone from Anne Hathaway to Katie Roiphe. Everywhere you look on the Internet you find self-appointed punishers at work. Never in human history has a system developed like the Internet, which allows for the free rein of our punishing instincts, conducted with complete anonymity, with no checks or balances, no moderation, and no accountability. On the Internet, our darkest evolutionary biology runs riot.

3

The Media Tried and Convicted Casey Anthony

Keith Long

Keith Long is an author, writer, and radio commentator.

In this fascinating viewpoint, the author describes how Casey Anthony—a young Florida woman accused of murdering her two-year-old daughter—was tried and found guilty in the media and on social media, before and after a jury found her not guilty of the crime. The author goes on to make a case—based on his own perusal of public records, talks with psychologists (none of whom had ever examined Anthony or any member of her family), and speculation—that Casey's father, George, was responsible for the crime. In the end, the author's article about trial by internet becomes an example of trial by internet!

The Casey Anthony trial became the most sensational news story of 2011. The Orlando, Florida court where the trial took place issued 600 press credentials, and *Time* magazine dubbed it the first social media trial of the century. The 22-year-old single mom was charged with three felonies including first degree murder, aggravated child abuse and manslaughter. When pictures surfaced on the internet showing her at a nightclub in June, 2008, shortly after her two-year-old daughter, Caylee, went missing, the media and public went ballistic. Thirty-one days passed after Caylee's

"The Media's Court of Public Opinion, Casey Anthony," by Keith Long. Reprinted by permission.

death before police were notified and then it was not mother Casey, but her family that called police and they were pointing fingers at her.

More time passed as thousands all over the country searched for the missing toddler. Finally, in December of that year the remains of the angelic Caylee were found in woods, just blocks from the young mother's home. During that time, images of the young mother partying, and her videotaped jailhouse interviews with parents consumed mainstream news and the social media blogosphere. Casey appeared concerned only about herself. None of the streaming images showed Casey Anthony with any apparent remorse or grief.

Today, her name remains synonymous with, "got away with murder," and it engenders animosity that is just as venomous today as it was during the investigation and trial. She was named the most unpopular person in America in 2011. Another poll in 2012 reinforced the public's collective disdain for her. The Casey Anthony trial was a public spectacle that came close in many respects to resembling the days of the Roman Colosseum, where the public thirsted to see lions devour the captured prize in their arena.

Social media transformed her three month courtroom trial into an arena of its own, and Casey Anthony was their prisoner. The trial's streaming videos and interactive blogs induced a frenzy that left the public demanding to see an embodiment of Caesar give his final "thumbs down" against their prize. Time magazine, one of many mainstream media publications that fed the court of public opinion during the trial said this: "Virtually no one doubts that Anthony was involved in her child's death," then added, "but if you see murder in Casey Anthony's big brown eyes during a live feed of her trial, you can tell all the world how delectable you will find her execution." Blogs exploded with conversations and opinions; cable news commentary announced "breaking news alerts" all blaming the mother, Casey Anthony, for the little girl's disappearance and death.

Florida's Attorney General, Pam Bondi, was interviewed by CBS news before the trial even started: "The evidence is overwhelming. No one else in the world except Casey Anthony could have done this." The *Chicago Tribune* reported, "Just when you think Casey Anthony cannot nauseate you anymore, try this: she wants more children." It was quite literally impossible to find a single reporter or media commentator, before and now even after her trial, who would say they thought this woman could be innocent.

We did find 12 jurors however who reached that conclusion. The jury was not sympathetic to the defendant. Many jurors cried as they voted to acquit. The prosecution's evidence was so thin they deliberated only 11 hours before finding her not guilty. So this sets up a very interesting difference of opinion. The jury was sequestered by order of the trial court and reached its decision based on evidence heard within the four walls of the courtroom. The public, on the other hand, had an information environment dominated by one point of view of this case. The media's court of public opinion was sustained by a carnival of pictures, videos, and opinion transmitted through blogs all over the internet. During the hour when the verdict was announced, 325,000 Tweets shouted 140-character screams of incredulity. A bare one per cent supported her acquittal. Tweets like this were the rule: "The jury was inept and lazy. That's why we have a baby killer being set free."

I am an investigative journalist who has become quite familiar with the Casey Anthony case. I can report an important part of my research has been focused on reaching an understanding of the public's perception of this story. I take every opportunity to sample reactions and opinions from waitresses, store clerks, professionals, and especially mothers. The mere mention of this former accused murderer's name stops conversations, interrupts tasks, and always evokes an immediate, visceral, and remarkably consistent reaction from virtually everyone I talk to.

Eyes roll; "Oh, that woman, I hate her. She got away with murder, no one would ignore her baby's disappearance for 31 days like she did." As I said, the opinions are virtually unanimous that

Casey Anthony is a horrid person. I inquire of reactions from people I casually meet for a simple reason: my research into the facts of the case has resolved itself into a conviction that the true story of Casey Anthony has yet to be told. The public has no clue what the real Casey Anthony story is about. Of course, she has barely breathed a word on her own behalf since her release, two years ago. So that is understandable.

Soon after the jury's "not guilty" verdict was announced, I had a conversation with Barry Sussman, the *Washington Post's* former Watergate editor for Woodward and Bernstein. He was then editor for Harvard's Media Watchdog program and he wanted my opinion on what the verdict would have been if the jury had not been sequestered. He described the reporting of this story as a media carnival. Barry invited me to write a centerpiece article for Harvard's Nieman Foundation for Journalism in November, 2011, only a few months after the verdict. My article broke records for reader response on the Harvard website.

Besides Barry, there were two other notable journalists who called out the pack journalism mindset that characterizes coverage of the story to this day. Howard Kurtz, host of CNN's "Reliable Sources" joined CNN's senior legal analyst, Jeff Toobin, in criticizing the media's coverage. Kurtz said, "I refused to join the media frenzy after two-year-old Caylee was killed." Kurtz added that what troubled him most was how the media turned the trial into entertainment. "It was great in terms of ratings, (but) I thought it was appalling in terms of the way it just seemed to take over the American media. The tone of the coverage was Casey Anthony must be guilty."

The defendant's lead defense attorney, Jose Baez, characterized the reporting as "media assassination." Kurtz added, "Let's be honest with ourselves: this is the exploitation of tragedy until it becomes entertainment. And that's why the situation is even worse than the indictment by Anthony's lawyer would suggest." Kurtz admitted that he winced at the onslaught of lawyers and psychologists on cable news channels and in blogs pontificating about the case:

"There were legal loudmouths who have gone on TV to convict Casey Anthony ... forgetting there is a difference between someone appearing guilty and the requirement that prosecutors prove guilt in a courtroom. Television has feasted off this case for three years." Kurtz shared his personal feelings admitting at one point he became so angry it made his blood boil. He was asked about his own Reliable Sources program coverage on CNN: "I stayed away from this." Kurtz refused to cover the story on his very popular CNN Sunday media discussion show. Kurtz's colleague at CNN, Jeff Toobin, shared his personal opinions in his usual, deadpan fashion: "Most of the coverage has been very hostile to Casey Anthony. The news media was very unfair to Casey Anthony."

These two highly regarded journalists, and Harvard's editor, Barry Sussman, are standard bearers who feel a responsibility to call for a return to a quality of journalism that originally inspired them to become journalists. They in turn, have inspired me to look beyond what we all see at the surface in this story. They inspired me to look beneath the surface and to find facts. I determined not to be persuaded by the media carnival we were all witness to, and many of us were part of.

Let me say at the outset, as a reporter, I see what everyone sees in this story. A young mother who knew early on that her daughter had disappeared. She lied to her parents, saying Caylee is with a nanny whom she named Zanny. Then 31 days later, after her own mother called police to arrest her, Casey lied to police, telling them "Zanny the nanny" said she had taken Caylee to teach Casey a lesson. Casey then lied about where the nanny lived, and even where Casey herself worked for the past two years. Police quickly discovered Casey hadn't held a job since shortly after her nearly three-year-old daughter, Caylee, was born. Investigators went to the apartment where Casey told them Zanny the nanny lived, and found it had been vacant for over six months; no one there ever heard of Zenaida Fernandez Gonzalez, the fantasy Zanny. Casey went to parties on weekends during the time Caylee was missing. She got a tattoo on her shoulder, "bella vita." Prosecutors characterized her as a party girl, who was seeking "the beautiful life," someone who wanted to be free from the responsibilities of being a mother to her daughter Caylee. In the court of public opinion it was all over: case closed!

In post trial analysis, I committed myself to follow the lead from those few journalists who called out the media coverage of the Casey Anthony trial. Jeff Toobin advised, "The media's coverage is something we should all discuss." So I now suggest the public and media need to take a breath. The time has come to have that conversation Jeff Toobin, Howard Kurtz and Barry Sussman ask for. I have researched trial evidence, statements of dozens of witnesses, and the family dynamic of the Anthonys living in the little home on Hopespring Drive, in Orlando. What I come away is the personal story of Casey Anthony, outlined here for the first time. My questions for the media, and its court of public opinion are these: Did police arrest the wrong person? Was the jury right when they said Casey Anthony was not guilty? Was Casey's mother, Cindy, involved in a cover up of a crime against her own granddaughter? If she was, who was Cindy protecting, Casey or Cindy's husband, George? I have the answers to these questions: yes, yes, yes, and George!

The first step to reach an understanding of Casey Anthony was obvious to me. I started with a fundamental question: What kind of a mother to Caylee was Casey Anthony? The answer came quickly and it left no doubt whatsoever. The top missing persons detective in the Orange County sheriff's department led the investigation of Caylee's disappearance. His name was Yuri Melich. He also testified as a primary witness for the prosecution during her trial. Melich and other detectives interviewed all of Casey's friends who knew her from the fourth grade until the day she was arrested. Melich focused on what her friends could say about Casey's behavior after Caylee was born, August 9, 2005. When the news broke of Casey's arrest, Casey's former friends abandoned her and distanced themselves from her. No one wanted to be associated with their former friend, Casey Anthony. So I looked at the multiple police interviews of these friends as an important source of information to confirm the kind of mother Casey was with Caylee. After all, none of her old friends wanted to defend this person who had been arrested and who was suddenly the prime suspect in the murder of her own daughter. Her friends were not immune to the community pressure blaming Casey. They were also aware that Casey was making headlines on news broadcasts, cable commentaries, and blogs all over the country. So I found it something more than surprising, and at the same time, significant, that all of her friends described Casey as an ideal mother.

Detective Melich's interview of Casey's friend, Melina Calabrese, was typical. As a close friend of Casey, Melina knew her well. She worked with Casey at Universal Studios and was close to her constantly from the first day Caylee was born. Melich asked Melina what kind of mother she knew Casey to be. Melich said, "Casey's relationship with Caylee from the time that you remember, how would you describe that relationship?"

Melina: "I had hoped for it to be mine. She and Caylee were adorable. I almost hoped for it you know because she was very good with Caylee. She gave Caylee almost everything a little girl could want. You know, Casey was very good with her. She just never raised her voice. Always you know, I never saw her touch her in a negative way. To this day, I hope my own mother-daughter bond is going to be like that. And it almost seemed easy."

All of the many police interviews of Casey's friends, associates, people she worked with, and her relatives, strongly reinforced Melina's statement to police: Casey was an ideal mother. No one could criticize or diminish Casey as a mother to Caylee. So it occurred to me, the criticisms of Casey's behavior as a mother to Caylee, all centered around her behavior after Caylee died, and especially the absence of grief Casey displayed after her daughter's death. How could a loving and doting mother not show and share her grief for the death of her beloved child?

For an investigative journalist, that begs the next important question: could Casey's bizarre behavior, lies, imaginary characters, and her inability to grieve, actually provide the missing insight into the mystery behind this young woman's story? That intriguing possibility led me to the next phase of my reporting. I began with a belief that whatever Casey's involvement may have been, the death of her two-year-old daughter, Caylee, was a traumatic experience. A consistent description from all her friends was that Casey and Caylee were literally inseparable. Casey cared for her constantly and loved her deeply. Her former fiance's father and a minister, Richard Grund, said it was obvious that Caylee gave Casey meaning in her life. So Caylee's death had to play a significant role in Casey's behavior. I believed the mystery of Caylee's death could be solved by understanding why Casey Anthony lied to police, why she made up a story about a fictitious Zanny the nanny? Also, I wanted to be able to report, how did Caylee die?

To answer these questions definitively, I sought out authorities in forensic psychiatry and studied case histories. I needed to know if Casey's behavior fit psychiatric models of post traumatic stress. I talked to experts in child trauma and family abuse. My research was always strictly anonymous. I was careful to not introduce polarization (or bias) into any discussion by mentioning her name, Casey Anthony into my conversations. I talked to PhD's, both psychologists and psychiatrists in order to get basic, generic answers to my questions. I described for them behavior similar to Casey's without mentioning her name. I wanted to test Casey Anthony's version of the events surrounding Caylee's death.

Casey Anthony laid out a detailed record of what she says happened the day Caylee died in interviews with three independent, court appointed experts -- two psychologists and one forensic psychiatrist -- all specialists in trauma and stress induced behavior. The record from two of these interviews was published after the trial at the order of the judge, Belvin Perry. The prosecution closely deposed both experts. During these intimate interviews, Casey talked extensively with these forensic experts about what happened the day Caylee died. She said her father woke her up from sleep holding Caylee's lifeless body, dripping wet from the backyard swimming pool and blaming her for the death. George ordered her to not say anything to her mother, Cindy. George then took Caylee's lifeless body away, telling Casey, "daddy will take care of things."

After reviewing and researching these depositions, I needed to know the answer to a simple, and seemingly incongruous question. Does Casey's inability to grieve, denial of her child's death, and need to protect her father who was responsible for her daughter's death ever occur in other women who experience the traumatic, sudden death of their young child? Has bizarre behavior like Casey's, such as denial, lack of grief, and lying ever been observed in the experience of these trauma specialists?

I asked psychologists and psychiatrists to describe reactions of a hypothetical young mother who was living in a severely dysfunctional home environment with her parents, and who then experiences the sudden, accidental death of her child, at the hands of her father. I asked them to consider such behavior assuming the father denies involvement in the death of her child, and tells the mother of the dead child to keep quiet about it. I included post trauma behavior such as denial, lying, and inability to grieve.

I wanted to know what kind of behavior forensic specialists would expect from a mother whose child died traumatically at the hands of her father, assuming she was raised in a severely dysfunctional family environment. The consensus reply was summarized by one well known PhD psychologist, Dr. William DeFoore, who has 30 years experience in counseling victims of trauma. He said, "In such a case as you describe, I would say that the young woman is caught in a trauma bond with her father." He went on to say that he would expect the daughter to deny the father's role in her daughter's death. I asked him to explain what he meant by this term, "trauma bond." He said, "In a trauma bond, the child is attached to the abusive, neglectful, abandoning parent because of her need for love and her subconscious belief that she will get love from her parent (father, in this case). Subconsciously, the young woman you describe is hoping for the love she never got--or only got on a minimal level."

At this point I measured the psychologist's description of "trauma bond" against Casey Anthony's behavior. Casey greeted her father in jail during his visits lovingly, saying, "you are the greatest father and grandfather in the world." Yet we know George had a seriously dysfunctional and dishonest relationship with Casey. We also know that Casey alleged George molested her beginning at age 8. So this explanation of a trauma bond could authoritatively explain the behavior of Casey, "after" Caylee's death.

It is quite obvious that not every woman whose child dies suddenly and traumatically at the hands of their father would go on to deny the death, and protect their father by inventing imaginary nannies and false explanations for the daughter's disappearance. The presumption in these remarks by the psychologist is that a young woman who behaves pathologically must at some level be living in a pathological family environment prior to the loss of her child. In other words, such reactions can occur when the young mother was already severely traumatized by her family environment, such as through incest and molestation by a close family member, like her father.

I then introduced the abuse element of Casey's version to the psychologist, again, without mentioning names. I said, suppose the woman we have been talking about grew up in a relationship where incest and abuse occurred at a young age. Then at age 19, the abused woman had her own child. Consider a scenario where her child accidentally died because of some action by the father. But the father denied both his abuse of his daughter and any role in her baby's death; I asked, how would you expect that woman to react?

Dr. DeFoore said something remarkable: "To acknowledge that her father not only abused her but is also responsible for the death of her child would destroy the possibility of her getting the love she wants. She has created a fantasy father, so that she can go on loving him. Her illusion of a fantasy father would be destroyed if she faced who he really is and what he has done."

The thousand pound elephant in the room throughout the entire backdrop of the Casey Anthony story of course is the Anthonys pathological family environment in their home on Hopespring Drive. The media blamed everything on Casey. The absence of grief, her lies, her imaginary job, all of her behavior created the denial and dysfunction so apparent in Cindy and George Anthony's behavior. However now it was beginning to appear that once again, the court of public opinion has it backwards. There is expert opinion that Cindy and George could have been responsible for the dysfunctional behavior that Casey suffered from, and not the other way around. In fact, I found all of this is well established in the psychiatric literature that abusive family environments can generate bizarre behavior in children who experience trauma such as the death of a child.

Cindy Anthony was a registered nurse who held a $1000 week management job at healthcare giant, Gentiva. She trained as a pediatric nurse. Yet with Casey seven months pregnant, sporting a huge baby bump and a belly button turned inside out, Cindy denied to everyone that Casey was pregnant. Casey's brother, Lee, asked his mother, "What is going on with Casey?" Cindy said to her 23-year-old son, "Let it go, Lee." Cindy's brother Rick, said, "What gives Cindy. You are a nurse for gosh sakes, everyone can see she is pregnant." Cindy told Rick he was wrong, "Casey is not pregnant." Cindy's colleagues at Gentiva saw Casey come by to see Cindy at work often and they asked Cindy about it. Cindy always denied her daughter's pregnancy to them. Cindy, though a professional nurse, never scheduled Casey for an Ob/Gyn exam.

Finally, just a few weeks before Caylee was born, Cindy had to admit Casey was about to deliver. Cindy went to the delivery room and arranged to have the nurses hand Caylee to Cindy first, before Casey held her. At delivery, George curiously positioned himself at the foot of his daughter's bed, almost it seemed, as a voyeur. The question occurs often in my research: did Cindy and

George worry that George was Caylee's father? I have answered that question in the affirmative.

George brought serious baggage to his marriage with Cindy. His first wife told Dr. Drew, the TV psychiatrist, that George was a genetic liar. George's anger management issues surfaced shortly after his marriage to Cindy when he threw his own father through a plate glass window, nearly killing him. George secretly stole $30,000 from Cindy's Gentiva retirement account, and then lost it all gambling. Of course he lied to Cindy (and the FBI) claiming for awhile he had been scammed by a Nigerian email ruse. George had an affair with a search volunteer while Caylee was still missing, and confessed to his involvement in Caylee's death during a private moment with her. Even the prosecutor, Jeff Ashton described George's misstatements as "George just being George."

George was by any measure, a horrible father to Casey. Hours after Caylee's body was discovered, George was called in for questioning by police. His first words to police were, "I am not changing my story." Police immediately searched the Anthony home again. George was frightened. He tried to commit suicide. In his suicide note, left just after Caylee was found, George apologized to wife Cindy and son Lee for his mistakes, but he could not bring himself to say anything to Casey.

All of the denial and dysfunction by the parents in the Anthony family, has been written off by the media and blogs as without a doubt, Casey's fault. One blogger said, "Casey Anthony represents the epitome of heartbreak that parenting adult children can bring. Herein lies one of the biggest problems I see for parents of adult children: They refuse to see the truth about their children."

My reporting disputes the media's court of public opinion on this critical point of who should be considered responsible for the pathological family environment Casey grew up in. There is no doubt, the abusive Anthony parents produced the behavior we witnessed in Casey Anthony.

The classic family dynamic for families with a father who molests one of their own children is well known. If the abuse is not reported and the victim does not receive support to face these crimes against her, both the abuser (father) and the non abusing parent (mother) typically deny the abuse ever happened; they blame the victim. The abused child cannot talk about her abuse. That is a description of the Anthony family dynamic in spades. Additionally, I could not find a single case history where an abused daughter grows up to have a child of her own, and then suffers the traumatic death of that beautiful child at the hands of her abusive father. So the combination of such horrible experiences suffered by Casey Anthony seems to be unprecedented.

The behavior of Casey Anthony, once the family dynamics are no longer denied and ignored, emerges as a textbook case history for a victim's reaction to unimaginable and horrible events at the hands of her own father, who she was trying to love. In the event, the media's court of public opinion has committed a serious injustice to this young woman. CNN's Jeff Toobin is right: "The news media owes an apology to Casey Anthony."

4

Google Tampers with Juries

Dominic Greive

Dominic Greive is an English Conservative politician and a member of the Queen's Privy Council. From May 2010 to July 2014, he was attorney general for England and Wales.

The ins and outs of the legal system as it applies to social media usage and internet mobs can be pretty complicated. In this viewpoint, excerpted from a speech given at the University of Kent in England in February 2013, the then UK attorney general sets out how social media and Google can compromise trial by jury. He cites prominent cases in the United States and the United Kingdom, in which improper use of media and the internet interfered with the administration of justice. He explains the legal meaning of "contempt" and demonstrates how certain internet practices by jurors fall into the category, and the law of contempt is flexible enough to apply to cover new media technologies.

As Attorney General I have various roles. I was once described as the "man with two hats". I have to say, I saw that description and thought – if only it was only two! Most, if not all, the hats I wear are non-political; that is to say, I act independently of the Government, and certainly do not act in a political manner: legal advice is legal advice, and must not be calibrated to political considerations.

"Trial by Google? Juries, Social Media and the Internet," Attorney General's Office and The Rt Hon Dominic Grieve QC, February 6, 2013. Licenced under the Open Government Licence v3.0. ©Crown Copyright.

Various aspects of the role of Attorney embody the rather broad notion of being "the guardian of the public interest". This includes having the ability to refer certain criminal cases to the Court of Appeal on the basis that the sentence imposed was "unduly lenient", being required to consent to certain criminal prosecutions – for example, terrorist offences which impact on the affairs of another jurisdiction, or prosecutions under the Official Secrets Act.

Being guardian of the public interest also encompasses enforcing the law of contempt. Contempt is, broadly speaking, a jurisdiction to protect the integrity of the judicial system and the courts. Just as the judicial system has many facets, so does the law of contempt.

And, as we shall see, the nature of contemporary contempt is changing, but the purpose of the law remains the same: in this context, it is to protect the right to a fair trial.

Allow me to illustrate the point with the assistance of another jurisdiction.

Late last month, the *Economist* ran a story about two senior federal prosecutors in Louisiana who resigned in disgrace when it was revealed that they were the source of vitriolic, anonymous blog posts directed at particular Federal judges.

Their resignation was followed by resignation of their boss, the United States Attorney for the Eastern District of Louisiana, a well respected man with a reputation for campaigning against political corruption and white collar crime.

The *Economist* said this: "The episode is a cautionary tale about the perils of the internet." Although many people think the anonymity that veils their online rants is absolute, plenty of jurisprudence argues otherwise...

The piece continued,

> Naturally, a host of federal targets – including some who have already pleaded guilty or been convicted – are now crying foul, saying the commenting amounted to a campaign to sway public opinion and poison the jury pool...

It is an interesting, disappointing story; one which I hope is never replayed by prosecutors in this jurisdiction.

But it illustrates vividly an important point: what we do on the internet does matter, and it is not only our jurisdiction which is concerned about the impact of the internet and social media on the right to a fair trial.

Just as defendants in the state of Louisiana are concerned that the jurors who convicted them may have been swayed by improper influence, we too must be careful to ensure that our juries are not improperly influenced, whether through published material they inadvertently encounter, or through conducting their own research – which I have termed "trial by Google" for tonight's purposes, for such research is usually internet-based.

The way our legal system mitigates those risks is through the law of contempt.

To think about this in more depth, I propose to cover:

- forms of contempt; in particular how the law of contempt protects the integrity of trial by jury

Contempt is a broad jurisdiction:

- It is the means by which certain court orders are enforced.

- It is the means by which judges regulate proceedings before them.

Contempt encompasses a summary jurisdiction, unique in our legal system, allowing judges to deal with certain matters as contempt in the face of the court.

It is more than a mere summary jurisdiction; as well as regulating what happens during proceedings in court, it covers what can be said about proceedings from outside court.

Some contempts are so serious that rather than dealing with it there and then, the judge refers it to me to consider bringing proceedings in the Divisional Court, part of the High Court.

The law of contempt regulates the behaviour of those involved in proceedings, including but by no means limited to, the jury.

As we shall see, the law relating to publication contempt and that relating to the conduct of jurors go hand in hand.

The Contempt of Court Act 1981 placed on a statutory basis what is known as the "strict liability rule". That rule provides that a publication – and it must be a publication for the strict liability rule to apply – may be in contempt of court, regardless of intent to do so, for conduct which tends to interfere with the course of justice.

The strict liability rule is limited by section 2(2) of the Act to apply only to,

> "a publication which creates a substantial risk that the course of justice in the proceedings will be seriously impeded or prejudiced..."

There is a defence to breaches of the strict liability rule in the following terms,

> "a person is not guilty of contempt of court under the strict liability rule in respect of a fair and accurate report of legal proceedings held in public, published contemporaneously and in good faith."

And finally, the rule only applies when proceedings are "active"; a concept about which, as I am sure you can imagine, much legal ink has been spilled over the past 30 years.

The 1981 Act was enacted following growing uncertainty about the scope of the former common law regime for strict liability contempt, which culminated in considerable criticism from the European Court of Human Rights in 1979 case *Sunday Times v UK*.

The Strasbourg Court held that an injunction obtained by the then Attorney against the *Sunday Times* to prohibit publication of an article breached its Article 10 rights.

Article 10, of course, guarantees the right to freedom of speech. It is a broad guarantee, and an extremely important one.

Freedom of speech, and its legal cousin, the open justice principle, feature in the legal system of any jurisdiction which respects the rule of law. Freedom of speech and the rule of law go hand in hand: both are certainly part of our proud common law heritage.

Freedom of speech encompasses not only the right of the media to speak, as it were, but also their right to gather material in order to exercise the right to free speech. It extends to the right of the public to be informed, by the media.

But it is not an unfettered right. Article 10(2) of the Convention provides that the right, "may be subject to such formalities, conditions, restrictions or penalties as are prescribed by law and are necessary in a democratic society, in the interests of national security, territorial integrity or public safety..."

The list goes on, and concludes with, "...maintaining the authority and impartiality of the judiciary."

And the judiciary, of course, includes the jury in a Crown Court trial. Article 6 of the Convention guarantees the right to a fair trial; again, a matter of heritage for our jurisdiction in any event.

So Parliament, seeking to balance these competing requirements, enacted the Contempt of Court Act 1981.

Far from being a restrictive enactment, the 1981 Act was intended to shift the balance of the law in favour of freedom of speech. It sought to clarify what could and could not be published about legal proceedings.

By clarifying the law, restrictions on publication were defined – and thereby limited – by the Act.

For example, section 4(2) of the Act allows a court to make an order postponing publication of certain reports of the proceedings until some future date or event. This is how the provision was described by Lord Denning in a leading case some time ago,

> "[The Contempt of Court Act] is not a measure for restricting the freedom of the press. It is a measure for liberating it. It is intended to remove the uncertainties which previously troubled editors. It is intended that the court should be able to make an order telling the editors whether the publication would be a contempt or not."

The paradigm example of this would be where there has been pre-trial legal argument, say to have the case thrown out as an abuse of process. Such argument would take place, of course, in the absence of the jury. It would be highly prejudicial, not to mention nonsensical, for a jury to be sent out of court during that argument, only to read about what happened in report of the proceedings the paper the following morning!

Or there may be several linked trials relating to the same crime: again, it would be highly prejudicial for the jury in one case to read of the evidence adduced in another. Of course, the same evidence may be common to both cases, but the manner in which it is adduced, the full context which will accompany it and the corresponding directions of the judge are vital components of the adversarial trial process.

Take away that context, and the evidence may assume an entirely different meaning. It was once said that if you take text out of context, all you are left with is a con, and I think there is some truth to that.

Underlying the strict liability rule is the recognition that the jury are entitled to – and will – read the papers, watch the news, and listen to the radio, and in doing so, encounter information about their cases, unless the judge directs otherwise. Parliament did not intend that jurors, or witnesses in the case, or even the judge, should be subjected to an automatic media blackout! If that was not the case, we would have a system of wholly secret justice.

Indeed, courts have a healthy realism about the integrity of jurors, their ability to focus on the evidence and to follow judicial directions. In 2006, the Court of Appeal said,

> "There is a feature of our trial system which is sometimes overlooked or taken for granted… juries up and down the country have a passionate and profound belief in, and a commitment to, the right of a defendant to be given a fair trial. They know that it is integral to their responsibility. It is, when all is said and done, their birthright…"

"We cannot too strongly emphasise that the jury will follow [the judge's directions], not only because they will loyally abide by the directions of law which they will be given by the judge, but also because the directions themselves will appeal directly to their own instinctive and fundamental belief in the need for the trial process to be fair."

However, it must be true that by framing so carefully what may or may not be said about legal proceedings in the 1981 Act, Parliament recognised that much harm could be done by juries encountering information that falls outside that framework.

Put simply, we are not to have trial by newspaper.

All this poses a question, a rather significant question: How does a legal regime framed when the internet was but a gleam in the eye of Tim Berners-Lee cope when faced with the flow of information that now forms the fabric of our culture?

More specifically, what does the internet mean for our system of trial by jury? Is the trial process equipped, or even able, to regulate the information that jurors receive? How can we be sure that jurors decide their cases on the basis of the evidence they hear and not what they looked up on their smart phones on the bus on the way to court?

To answer these questions, I will first consider two contempt cases I brought under the strict liability rule, before moving to address juror misconduct under contempt of court at the common law.

One of the first contempt cases I brought since coming to Office was that relating to the trial of a Ryan Ward. It was, the Divisional Court noted, the first time an internet-based contempt had been referred to them.

Mr Ward faced trial for murder in Sheffield Crown Court. The case had received a considerable degree of local publicity. It was the prosecution case that the defendant had murdered the victim following a gallant attempt he made to intervene in an attack by the defendant against a woman. The nature of Mr Ward's defence, self defence and the absence of murderous intent, meant that the need for the media to abide by their obligations under the strict liability rule was as important as ever.

The jury was addressed by the trial judge in the following terms,

> "Also, I would imagine by the nature of this case, and you'll see there's obviously press interest in it, there will be some reporting of this case. Again that's a matter the press are free to report upon but you go on only the evidence you hear in this room, not the view other people may or may not have about it."

He added another warning:

> "Please don't try and get information from outside this room about this case. Don't, for example, consult the Internet, if there is anything out there on it. I'm not saying for one moment there is but don't go there, don't try and get it from anywhere else…"

During the early evening of the first day of the trial, the *Daily Mail* published an article under the headline, "Drink-fuelled attack: Ryan Ward was seen boasting about the incident on CCTV, alongside a photograph of the defendant holding a pistol with his finger on the trigger. The photograph remained accessible on the *Daily Mail* website for just under five hours; it was removed following a request from the police.

In the early hours of the following morning, the *Sun* published the same photograph on its website and in its print edition. The photograph in the print edition was cropped to conceal the gun; the online version was partially cropped, but that the defendant was holding a gun remained clear from the photograph. The photograph was taken down that evening, again following a request from the police.

When the matter was brought to the trial judge's attention, he carefully asked whether any of the jury had seen the articles or the photographs. They had not. The case continued and Mr Ward was convicted of murder.

I brought proceedings for contempt. In this case, each defendant publisher conceded that publication of the photograph was wrong, and attributed the mistake to innocent error. But each

– unsuccessfully – argued that the photograph did not create a substantial risk of serious prejudice.

The Divisional Court found the case to be proved; there was a substantial risk that a juror trying the case would see the photograph and be prejudiced by it. Each paper was fined £15,000 with £28,000 costs.

Far from highlighting any inability of the law to deal with internet contempt matters the Ward case clarifies, helpfully in my view, how the strict liability rule applies to internet publications, and what the consequential expectations on publishers are.

And although the two publications involved may not have welcomed the ruling, I think the clarity brought by the judgment has been welcomed by the media.

Such clarity was, after all, was one of the reasons which lay behind the enactment of the 1981 Act.

Shortly after bringing that case, I brought proceedings against the publishers of the *Sun* and the *Mirror* for their vilification of a man named Chris Jefferies during the investigation into the tragic death of Joanna Yeates in late 2010. It was clear from the outset of the press coverage during the investigation that the media "had their man". Chris Jefferies was later to say that he became a household name, "for all the wrong reasons".

There was nothing particularly new with this type of coverage; the media "feeding frenzy" is by no means a modern phenomenon. What was striking about the case was the rigour with which Mr Jefferies was pursued by the media during the period when the strict liability rule in the 1981 Act was supposed to be engaged.

The coverage sought to portray Mr Jefferies as plainly responsible for the death of the victim, associated him with allegations of child abuse, and referred to him as an "oddball".

A melodramatic side piece titled, "1974 strangler never caught", declared ominously "Last night police refused to rule out a link between the two killings" (which is hardly surprising: find me a single officer who will categorically rule out a connection between two similar unsolved crimes in the same area!). Another headline read, "The Nutty Professor" above a banner stating, "Bizarre past of Joanna Yeates murder suspect".

The contempt was proved. What was interesting about the decision of the Divisional Court was that, not only did it consider the residual impact of the extreme publicity on any eventual juror, it also considered that the extent of the vilification may have deterred witnesses on behalf of Mr Jefferies, had he been charged, from coming forward, for fear of being associated with such an obviously guilty man.

Of course, not only was Mr Jefferies never charged, another man altogether was later convicted of the murder and sentenced to life imprisonment with a minimum term of 20 years.

So it is clear that the law of contempt does not permit trial by newspaper, whether that is in the print or online editions.

But neither does the law of contempt permit trial by Google.

(Of course, I say Google, I mean any internet search platform, Bing, Yahoo, Wikipedia, Twitter, Facebook, blogs, the list goes on…)

And this brings me onto common law contempt.

Common law contempt is intentional contempt. It is conduct which tends to undermine the administration of justice, done with the intention of undermining the administration of justice.

All juries are directed in robust terms about the need not to conduct their own research into the case. These robust instructions reflect the gravity of a juror's task. Indeed, it is hard to think of a more serious or important civil duty that virtually any member of the public may be called upon to conduct.

It has always been necessary to direct jurors not to discuss the case with anyone, not to visit the scene of the crime, not to research the witnesses or defendant details. And now such directions extend to not researching the case on the internet.

To ignore those directions, intentionally, amounts to a contempt of court.

Intention, of course, is different to motive. While you may not desire, for example, to derail a trial, the law considers that by embarking on a course of conduct that is virtually certain to derail a trial, you have intended to bring about that result.

Before getting into the detail, a word about the internet and the law: am I trying to reconcile the irreconcilable?

It is often said that the system of trial by jury was the bulwark of our democracy, a bastion of freedom.

While few would dispute describing trial by jury in such terms, I wonder if for many it would seem more natural to describe the internet in that way: for many, the internet is now the champion of freedom. The connectivity it provides has gone some considerable way towards uniting the world as a global village. The role of social media in the Arab Spring uprisings is well documented.

The internet is surely, the argument goes, an unstoppable force for good?

Taking the argument a little bit further, in contrast to the liberation provided by the internet, we have the law; a rigid framework that is dour, unresponsive, and above all, lacks understanding of the changing role of technology in society.

I do not accept the premise of either assertion.

Certainly the internet has been and is a champion of freedom, and has played an important part in opening up some societies, and helping to achieve social change.

And certainly there have been times when the law has been unable to adapt to modern society, and those responsible for making the law have been unable to see the need for the law so to adapt.

But I want to argue this evening that the law of contempt is both adaptable and resilient in the face of the challenges of technology.

The strict liability rule very deliberately only applies to information which presents a substantial risk of serious prejudice or impedance.

About many criminal trials, there may be all kinds of prejudicial information "out there" on the internet. This could be in the form of archived news reports about the defendant's previous court appearances, or it could be, to use the words of the old authorities in a modern context, mere chaff and banter about the case on someone's Facebook page or Twitter feed.

The strict liability rule can be fairly relaxed about such material – it is unlikely to present a substantial risk of serious prejudice because it is a needle buried away in the haystack of the internet. (I say the strict liability rule can be fairly relaxed – it can be, but is not always!)

Indeed, most publishers are very careful not to link reports of live cases to archived news reports about the same defendant.

So the chances of a juror seeing such material are fairly slim, providing they haven't gone looking for it. So, to use the words of Article 10(2) of the Convention, in view of those risks, attempting to purge the internet of all such material would not be "necessary in a democratic society".

Trial by Google, however, is different.

The reason is this: I mentioned a moment ago that the internet is a haystack of material, scattered with the odd prejudicial needle, as it were. Trial by Google allows a juror to locate the haystack, find the needle, pull it out and ascribe significance to it that it simply would never have had otherwise.

It takes a minor risk and turns it into a major risk.

In doing so, trial by Google offends some foundational principles of our legal system.

The first principle is that a conviction, or for that matter an acquittal, should be based on evidence adduced in court, in accordance with established rules of evidence, subject to the supervision of the judge.

Let's say a defendant being tried for grievous bodily harm had previously been tried — and acquitted – of rape. Let's say the case against the defendant for GBH does not feature details of the rape allegations. And with good reason too: the strict rules of evidence relating to bad character do not allow that kind of highly prejudicial material to be adduced in the circumstances of this case. Even if the rape acquittal was admissible, the judge would have explained the relevance of the bad character evidence in careful terms. The jury trying the defendant are to base their verdict on the evidence adduced before them; the previous acquittal was excluded for good reason. Let's say the judge has admitted some so-called bad character evidence, but that he was very careful in the way he crafted the directions to the jury about how it is relevant.

Now, let's say one of the jury decide to take matters into their own hands by looking up archived news reports about the defendant – in defiance of the judge's directions not to do that very thing.

Before too long, a bit of internet searching reveals that this is not the first time the defendant had been before the courts, and that he had in fact faced trial for rape. The rest of the jury must be told, the juror says to herself! There is information about the defendant that the judge is trying to withhold from us!

From this point onwards, the trial process is undermined.

The jury will no longer be able to deliver a verdict based solely on the evidence adduced before them; the role of the judge has been usurped, the defendant's right to a fair trial is prejudiced. The press, who had been scrupulous in their reporting of the GBH matter, avoiding all mention of the defendant's previous convictions, might as well have not bothered. The defendant may not have been tried by newspaper, but he was certainly tried by Google!

Of course, it is often hard to tell if the above research has been carried out, which leads us to the next fundamental objection to trial by Google:

Trial by Google offends the principle of open justice.

It should be clear to the defendant, the public, the victim and the prosecution what the evidence in the case is. If a jury is exposed to prejudicial material which, for whatever reason, is not before the court, the basis on which the defendant is convicted or acquitted will never be known.

The principle of open justice is met by our system of trial by jury through proceedings being in open court, through the adversarial scrutiny of the evidence, and through the judge's directions to the jury before they retire to consider their verdict. All this is undermined by trial by Google.

A further facet of the principle of open justice is that evidence can be challenged, probed and questioned. Open justice is scrutinised justice. By definition, that is not so with trial by Google; not only is the basis of the jury's finding unclear, but the parties will have been denied any opportunity to challenge the evidence which the jury itself gathered.

This returns us to our original question: is the law of contempt fit for purpose?

After all, we live in an information age. Searching for information about something we are unsure of is second nature for many; how can the law expect jurors to do something different? Surely only Mr. Justice Canute would seek to stem the flow of the tide of information in this way?

Well the law can, and does, expect jurors to show restraint. The principles which underlie this expectation are nothing new.

All that is new is that there is an additional area in which jurors are required to show restraint.

The fundamental principles underlying the need for juror restraint are timeless.

The scenario I described a moment ago involving a juror searching for material about the defendant on the internet was, sadly, not fictitious. The juror's name was Theodora Dallas and the defendant was called Barry Medlock. The trial was at Luton Crown Court in 2011.

For conducting her searches which revealed the previous acquittal of the defendant for rape, Dr. Dallas was found by the Lord Chief Justice to be in contempt of court, and was committed to 6 months' imprisonment. Barry Medlock had to be retried before a fresh jury, and the victim had to give evidence again.

When passing sentence on Dr. Dallas, the Lord Chief Justice said;

> "Jurors who perform their duties on the basis that they can pick and choose which principles governing trial by jury, and which

orders made by the judge to ensure the proper process of jury trial they will obey, or who for whatever reason think that the principles do not apply to them, are in effect setting themselves up above the jury system and treating the principles that govern it with contempt…"

The Lord Chief Justice went on to underline that the court's robust approach was not borne out of lack of understanding of the significance and role of the internet.

"Judges, no less than anyone else, are well aware of and use modern technology in the course of their work. The internet is a modern means of communication. Modern technology and means of communication are advancing at an ever increasing speed. We are aware that reference to the internet is inculcated as a matter of habit into many members of the community, and no doubt that habit will grow. We must however be entirely unequivocal."

Pausing there for a moment, I think I should highlight that it was our current Lord Chief Justice who, in December 2010, first permitted the use of live, text-based communication from the court room, initially on an interim basis, and later on a settled basis.

The allegation that the judiciary do not understand the internet is simply without merit.

Returning to the Dallas case, the Lord Chief Justice continued, "The problem therefore is not the internet: the potential problems arise from the activities of jurors who disregard the long established principles which underpin the right of every citizen to a fair trial."

I endorse those remarks.

Indeed, the internet has made the commission of many criminal offences much easier. It would be absurd to suggest that such conduct should no longer be criminalised on account of the ease with which such offences can now be committed.

Given the focus of my remarks has been on the need to prevent jurors from accessing prejudicial material, advertently or inadvertently, I have not spent time examining the potential for jurors to use the internet to communicate with defendants, or indeed witnesses, using the internet.

That is not so much trial by Google, but rather trial by Facebook Friend Request. That the law is apt to deal with such irregularities was demonstrated in the case of Frail and Sewart where a juror, Frail, initiated contact with a defendant, Sewart, whom she had just acquitted. The contact was made while the jury was still deliberating the guilt of the remaining defendants in what had been a long, multi-handed organised crime trial.

Details of the jury's deliberations were revealed by Frail in the course of a Facebook chat she initiated with Sewart. In doing so, Fraill breached the prohibition against that very thing contained in section 8 of the 1981 Act, in addition to breaching the directions of the judge not to go on the internet to research the case.

Both denied the allegations, and a trial took place before the Lord Chief Justice, who, sitting with two High Court Judges, found the case proved.

Sewart was sentenced to two months' imprisonment, suspended for two years, on account of her young child and the fact that she had already spent 14 months on remand prior to her acquittal. Frail received a term of 8 months' immediate custody.

I mention the case as I conclude because it further demonstrates the flexibility of the existing legal framework law to this very modern form of offending. Save for a brief discussion at the contempt trial about the true meaning of LOL – opinions vary – there could have been no allegations that there was any lack of appreciation in the court room of the impact of modern technology on the trial process, nor what to do about it.

[...]

I hope that I have demonstrated that the legal framework for the jury trial in this jurisdiction starts from the premise that the jury are to be trusted, and establishes a framework in which their vital function is to flourish, and be preserved.

We have never allowed trial by newspaper; and neither do we allow trial by Google.

The *Economist* article I outlined earlier concluded with the exhortation to the new United States Attorney for the Eastern District of Louisiana to, and I quote, "stay out of the chat rooms".

I can only conclude by imploring jurors in this jurisdiction to do likewise.

5

Witch Hunts Don't Presume Innocence

Crime Talk

The website Crime Talk is operated by a self-described 24-year-old psychology graduate and aspirating crimefighter who writes about criminal justice and criminal psychology.

Trial by media and trial by internet are nothing new. In this piece, the author traces the roots of the phenomenon to the witch trials of the Middle Ages and in Salem, Mass., in the 1600s. Readers will also find some important questions about how the principle of "innocent until proven guilty" should be applied in the absence of formal charges or a traditional trial. Additionally, the author raises the question of—in the cases of accusations of sexual abuse in particular—where we draw the line between respecting those who say they've been sexually abused and respecting the rights of those who have been accused.

E arly last month, YouTuber Toby Turner, AKA Tobuscus, was subject to a number of allegations by a former girlfriend, April Fletcher. These allegations ranged from Turner's own drug abuse to serious accusations that he both drugged and raped April while they were together. For those unaware, Turner has a YouTube subscriber count across his channels of around 15 million – he is incredibly popular; He is also the latest in a series of prominent male YouTubers to be accused of sexual assault through a social media platform.

"Trial by Media, Trial by Internet," by Crime Talk, WordPress, May 31, 2016. Reprinted by permission.

In this current climate of unlimited broadband, smartphones and social media, the internet seems to have metamorphosed into a whole separate world, larger than our own tangible one, and governed by an entirely different set of rules. Where once a person's actions were only important to a tiny fragment of the human population, now they can be judged by millions of people, sitting behind keyboards, in every corner of the globe. And this is what inevitably happens when someone as high profile as Turner is subject to sexual allegations over social media. The trial plays out over the internet rather than in a court room.

The term 'trial by media' was coined relatively recently, 'trial by social media' even more so. These phrases describe a phenomenon that can be loosely traced back to way before the birth of any form of media, to the 'witch-hunt'. The mass hysteria surrounding witchcraft, particularly in Europe during the middle ages and during the Salem Witch trials, provides a cautionary tale about how moral panic can lead to false accusations and failure to follow due process. The strongly held belief and fear of someone's guilt could become so widespread, that any evidence to the contrary was quashed and that actual guilt or innocence no longer mattered. During the middle ages a 'witch-hunt' could lead to an execution; nowadays it is not physical damage that is inflicted, but rather damage to one's reputation. The modern day 'witch-hunt' is a trial by media, a 'social media witch-hunt' where the accused is determined as guilty, not on evidence, not based on charges brought against them, but based on sensationalism by anyone with a keyboard.

The reaction to the Toby Turner rape allegations has been predictably substantial, specifically across non-mainstream media platforms or social media. It is hardly surprising that someone who made their name on the internet, is held accountable by it. The general conversation has rightly been supportive towards the alleged victim, and has led to wider conversation about the nature of power-imbalance within relationships and sexual assault as a whole. However, there is a flip side. Whilst these conversations are undoubtedly positive; belief in the survivor's story can naturally manifest as a belief in the accused's guilt and, when the trial is being held by social media, irreparable damage to their reputation.

Continuously through this discussion online, 'innocent until proven guilty' has been shouted across the internet by either those who believe Turner to be innocent, or those who place weight on the principle. The US legal system is built on the presumption of innocence, all trials are based on the premise that people are innocent until proven guilty. But how does this work when there isn't a traditional trial? How does this work when a story breaks on the internet, and the punishment is dealt out by millions of usernames on a screen with the ability to make or break a reputation?

Turner's case is merely an example of the 'trial by media' phenomenon. The accusations against him have not made it into mainstream media, nor have any charges been brought against him (to the best of my knowledge). His situation is vastly different to many others' that could be discussed; but is reflective of a trend, where accusations against persons are so sensationalised and publicised, that maintaining a presumption of innocence is increasingly difficult as everyone taps their keyboards to have their say. Maybe the courts haven't tried this person, but the public has.

This trend is particularly prominent in cases where people are accused of sexual abuse, where there is so much importance placed on believing the victim, that presuming the innocence of the accused falls second. It's a difficult and contentious area, and one worthy of further discussion. The importance of believing victims who come forward in these cases is indisputable, regardless of whether it is to the police or over social media; however, with increasingly microscopic media coverage, public outrage, and in some cases mass hysteria, do we also have an obligation to protect the accused from a presumption of guilt and prevent a potential 'witch-hunt'?

6

You'll Always Be Guilty Online

Sarah A. Downey

Sarah A. Downey is a writer, lawyer, privacy advocate, and advisor to Abine, an online privacy company.

This article offers a close look at some of the personal consequences of misinformation or out-of-date information circulating on the internet. Author Sarah Downey points out how the First Amendment to the Constitution makes it difficult to force newspaper and website owners to unpublish news reports of arrests, even if the courts have dropped all charges and expunged the arrest from an individual's record. In addition to acknowledging the conflict, this piece offers some suggestions for compromise.

More and more people are having "Google problems." They usually look like this: a) someone got arrested; b) the local newspaper wrote about it; c) prosecutors dropped the charges completely; d) the person's record was expunged (in other words, the slate was wiped clean); but e) the original arrest article, however, is still online.

Now whenever anyone searches that person's name, the arrest is one of the top Google results even though they weren't guilty.

"Online, You Are Guilty Even After Being Proven Innocent," by Sarah A. Downey, Abine, May 20, 2011. Reprinted by permission.

Google: Your New Permanent Record

You can imagine the trouble this causes for the individual seeking the article's takedown: difficulty getting a job, a promotion, or even a date. It seems unfair that even though the judicial system saw fit to remove all traces of the arrest from the person's record, there's no corresponding requirement that the local newspaper do the same. What's the point of expunging a record when anyone with internet access can bring up an old, bogus arrest? Even if a court of law drops the matter, the court of public opinion has condemned that person for life.

The Free Speech Rights of Publishers Trump Those of Individuals

In the battle of the newspapers versus the individual's reputation, the law is on the newspapers' side. They have a First Amendment right to report true information and are under no legal obligation to remove—"unpublish," as it's referred to lately—content, even when significant updates have occurred. In our experience, publishers are generally unwilling to remove articles that were factually accurate when written. Their reasoning ranges from lofty (saying they don't want to "rewrite the historical record") to lazy (they have a policy of never changing anything).

Some publications *will* remove an article, but only if the stars align and several factors exist: the publication doesn't have a strict policy against unpublishing, we reach an actual human being, we reach an actual human being *who's in a good mood that day*, we're able to provide documentation of the dropped charges or expunged record, and the person to whom we speak decides that the facts of the particular situation warrant removal. It takes hard work, persistence, and luck. Does it happen? Yes, but you can see why it's pretty rare.

How Courts Have Handled the Unpublishing Problem

Recognizing the damage that a negative online article can do to someone's reputation, defense attorneys have requested court orders that newspapers unpublish arrest stories about their clients after they're found innocent. The few courts that have issued such orders, however, quickly rescinded them in the face of First Amendment challenges. Simply put, *you can't censor a newspaper's free speech rights to protect your client's privacy.*

The only research that the publishing industry has conducted on this issue shows a lack of uniformity in opinion and response to requests to unpublish. (To read more, check out Kathy English's report, "The Longtail of news: To unpublish or not to unpublish"). One thing is clear: this issue is only becoming more relevant as the internet replaces print publications. How do the First Amendment rights of publishers stack up against the privacy rights of the accused, and how should courts and the publishing industry treat this balance in the future?

Search engines and content providers, like online newspapers, should recognize their critical role as gatekeepers of information. They should listen to and consider individual situations, even if they're not obligated to do so. Sure, a 20 year-old article about an arrest may be *factually accurate,* but is it really *fair* to leave it up when it's not newsworthy and makes it impossible for a person to move on in his or her life? Each case is a balancing act, and a quality publication will analyze the pros and cons, not automatically refuse to help.

Dealing With Unpublishing Requests: Fair Compromises & Solutions

Here are a few compromises and solutions we'd like to see publishers and content providers use more often:

Implement a sunsetting or le droit a l'oubli system: Sunsetting is an automated system used by publishers that retires articles about arrests after a certain preset period. It programs sites to forget, essentially giving content an expiration date. Just like human memory, sunsetting ensures that some things don't persist forever.

Block the article from being indexed by search engines: Use a robots.txt file to prevent search engines from crawling and indexing the site in search results. The article will stay up on the newspaper's website, but it won't be nearly as visible (or as harmful) if it's not on the search engines.

Remove or anonymize names, especially for lesser crimes: A publisher can maintain the integrity of an article while protecting individual privacy by removing or anonymizing a person's name (for example, changing it to "Doe"). The publication BloomU Today takes this approach "if the offense is minor and not a felony charge."

Unpublish the entire article: A rare solution that many publishers consider extreme, removing an entire article may be warranted when it is particularly old, irrelevant, inaccurate, or dangerous to an individual's privacy or safety.

Add an update or editorial note: Sometimes all an individual wants is an edit at the bottom of an article updating or correcting the unwanted information, and for the most part, publishers are not resistant to do so. This solution, however, has limited practical effect: a reader has to scroll to the bottom to find the edit, and by that point the damage has usually been done. It also has no effect on search results.

We're optimistic that publishers will adopt these gray-area solutions as we see more and more cases where people's online identities hold back their real-life identities.

7

You Can Survive an Internet Trial

Michael Roberts

*Michael Roberts is a licensed private investigator, digital &
social forensic analyst, and internet litigation support consultant
with Rexxfield.com and Page1.me. He specialises in identifying
anonymous internet antagonists and online reputation repair services.*

*In the following viewpoint, Michael Roberts shares his personal
experience with what he calls "internet libel" to show readers how
it can happen, how significant the damage can be, and how difficult
it is to repair. Fortunately, Roberts, an information security and
IT forensics expert, was able to use his experience to become a
specialist in the repair of online reputations. Here he offers advice
and workable solutions for repairing the damage caused by internet
libel and related crimes.*

There is a "low-tech" form of personal injury that goes largely
unnoticed by those yet to experience it, and yet causes
billions of dollars in irreparable damage to business goodwill,
personal reputation and very significantly the emotional well-
being of victims. This assault is called *INTERNET LIBEL*; a
form of the ancient legal theory of *SLANDER* with origins in
Roman jurisprudence.

A person who relies on his or her reputation to find gainful
employment or to find and retain customers, is particularly

susceptible to a malicious smear campaign. His or her livelihood can be as thoroughly destroyed by a relentless and anonymous blogger as that of a farmer who has had his livestock destroyed and barns set aflame by a vandal. The difference being that judges can relate to a tangible loss of $500,000 worth of cows and corn, but may dismiss the libel victim's intangible losses as petty, and not worthy of setting in motion the wheels of justice.

I personally survived such an assault; it was a frustrating and bitter experience, which left a business in ruins, staff unemployed and vendors unpaid. By the grace of God I was able to turn this adversity into an opportunity by combining my experience in information technology security and forensics with my experiences in combating the libelous siege against my character. This combination manifested in the form of "Rexxfield". By collaborating with experts from various fields, including psychology, medicine, technology, legal and public relations, we were able to produce resources to assist victims in their efforts to remedy the wrongs and for potential victims to mitigate the risks.

In law, libel is the written communication of a statement that makes a false or deceptive claim, expressly stated or implied to be factual, that may harm the reputation of an individual, business, product, group, government or nation. Most jurisdictions allow legal actions, civil and/or criminal, to deter various kinds of defamation and retaliate against groundless criticism. Related to defamation is public disclosure of private facts where one person reveals information which is not of public concern and the release of which would offend a reasonable person. Unlike libel or slander, truth is not a defense for invasion of privacy.

Despite the misunderstanding by many Americans, slander and libel (defamation) are not protected forms of free speech under the US First Amendment.

Very little has been done to assess the cost or stimulate moves toward equitable judicial reforms to combat internet libelers who are simply low technology cyber stalkers, antagonists, liars, extortionists and emotional terrorists. One well-placed blog entry or web site with strategically placed keyword combinations can destroy an individual's career, or many years of reputation and goodwill for a business. For this unethical and cowardly minority a single blog can mean the end of his or her victim's career; or the livelihood of a few people or thousands of families who depend on the continued good standing of their employer in the community.

Although there is legislation for criminal prosecution of defamation offenders in some U.S. jurisdictions (18 US states), it is almost unheard of. This leaves only civil court action, which is expensive, drawn out, and emotionally draining.

The explosive increase in public hotspots in restaurants, airports and other anonymous Internet connections, makes anonymity easier by the day. Additionally, the third-party dissemination and republication of libel can turn reputation problems into a wildfire. This can be particularly damaging if the victim has a unique name or trademark and a low appearance density in search engines. The dilemma is exacerbated further due to the fact that many web sites refuse to take down libelous materials without a court order.

Rumors of Your Internet Anonymity Have Been Greatly Exaggerated

The lie mongers engage in guerrilla tactics and wield their poisonous keystrokes with what they believe to be impunity by hiding behind anonymous user names, guest passes and I.P cloaking solutions. For those of you in these miscreants' sights, they appear impossible to catch, but there is hope!

I have had extensive personal experiences with an antagonist who had relentlessly attacked me physically, emotionally, financially and publicly. Free Internet blogs have been the most damaging venues to me as an entrepreneur; in early 2008 I had an agreement in principal with a European angel investment team to fund a start-up venture that I could not grow organically. Within 24 hours of the agreement the angels found my antagonist's libelous web site and withdrew their offer immediately. A little later, in early April 2008, a $70 million enterprise was enthusiastically engaged in dialogue with me for a partnering venture in the USA… until they found *"that web site"* and withdrew from the venture. (My antagonist has been jailed subsequently for unrelated matters.)

Naturally, the more absurd the assertions the less likely an intelligent and objective observer will be to believe it. However, once that bystander becomes a potential employer or strategic partner the scenario changes drastically. The decision they make about associating with a libel victim will be filtered by the question "what will my customers think?" If your antagonists are clever, they will cast flaming aspersions against you that are altogether deceptive, but sprinkled with a little truth that, although innocent in its own right, makes the tale all the more believable. This is called "spin."

Basic Requirements of a Defamation Case

A defamation plaintiff must usually establish the following elements to recover damages:

Identification The plaintiff must show that the publication was "of and concerning" himself or herself.

Publication The plaintiff must show that the defamatory statements were disseminated to a third party.

Defamatory Meaning The plaintiff must establish that the statements in question were defamatory. For example, the language must do more than simply annoy a person or hurt a person's feelings.

Falsity The statements must be false; truth is a defense to a defamation claim. Generally, the plaintiff bears the burden of proof of establishing falsity.

Statements of Fact The statements in question must be objectively verifiable as false statements of fact. In other words, the statements must be provable as false. (Caveat: Expressions of opinion can imply an assertion of objective facts. See *Milkovich v. Lorain Journal.*)

Damages The false and defamatory statements must cause actual injury or special damages.

Do Not Fight Fire With Fire

In doing so you are simply going to inspire your antagonist to double his or her efforts. This is even more likely if the offender has a narcissistic or anti-social personality disorder such as the person obsessed with ruining every aspect of what used to be my very normal and boring life. By not fighting back you remove the sociopath's source of glee; the air these people breathe is the outward manifestation of your torment. In the same way a cat will stop playing with a mouse when it plays dead, a sociopath will grow bored if he or she is unable to elicit painful reactions from a victim. As tempting as it may be to fight back, the best thing you can do with this type of person is humble your pride and opt for a strategic withdrawal; that's right; DISENGAGE! However, this does not mean you should give up, because your reputation will not get any better through inaction. A victim simply needs to be careful and undertake remedial actions "under the radar" thus denying a sociopath his/her reward. Rexxfield has perfected many ways of achieving these objectives.

My father is a simple but wise man; I remember him once saying of some bullies who taunted and lied about me in grade four *"what they say let them say."* I responded, *"but some kids believe them!"* He replied *"the truth will remain the truth no matter how it is believed."* As it turned out I settled the issue with one of the two fights I have had in my life (both under the age of 12); but the fact remains that truth does remain the truth despite what Mr. Plato may think.

A Response to Internet Libel & Smear Campaigns

As mentioned, don't waste time fighting back; you will only fuel the fire. Seek injunctive relief through the courts by all means if the case is watertight, obvious and potentially affordable. If you can't afford court, try the steps below:

1st step – Give Libel Notice to the Antagonist

Give formal notice to the libeler of his/her libel. This leaves them without excuse should you seek damages through court. You have an obligation to mitigate your damages as it is within your reasonable power to do so. But be careful of the Narcissists described above.

2nd step – Give Libel Notice to the 3rd Party Publisher

Blog and forum owners don't want to get dragged into a street fight or a court battle (although in the USA and Europe they are generally immune to liability). Although the law is somewhat unclear as to the extent of 3rd party providers and re-publishers of information and differs country to country, I found that in many cases, the site owners quickly removed the anonymous postings made by my antagonist when I provided them with very basic proof of libelous claims. Once they have been formally provided with proof of libel they are often reasonable; there are plenty of jack-assess too.

3rd Step – Dilution is the Key

The best strategy is to push the offensive and libelous material off the first page of Google and as far from the top of the list as practicable. If the libel has already occurred it will be relatively easy to design your response; simply analyze the keyword strategy used by your antagonist and do a better job.

Chances are most people or organizations will not consider an online libel campaign as a serious risk to their future until an enemy has laid siege to their Google ramparts.

Many organizations today are investing heavily in Search Engine Optimization (SEO) campaigns using internal efforts as well as massive outsourcing contracts with SEO specialists. I strongly suggest that if you are implementing an SEO campaign, do it properly and incorporate an effective libel mitigation strategy. Chances are you can piggyback it on your general SEO marketing strategy for no or little extra cost; it will prove to be a prudent and economical insurance policy. In addition, an SEO vendor who understands the need for potential libel litigation is likely to be a more capable SEO practitioner.

For Organizations

Search engine optimization (SEO) is the process of improving the volume and quality of traffic to a web site from search engines via "natural" ("organic" or "algorithmic") search results for targeted keywords. Usually, the earlier a site is presented in the search results or the higher it "ranks", the more will be the searchers visiting that site.

Incorporating libel litigation considerations into SEO often involves using keyword combinations which are not presently important but may be in the future as a result of bad press, smear campaigns, critiques, email chain letters and so forth. The most obvious contingency being the names of key individuals in an organization who may not necessarily have a high public profile now, but may be thrust into the limelight if named (rightly or wrongly) in a scandal, accident or other unfortunate event.

For Individuals

My personal testimony with regard to online libel is mortifying. The allegations that were leveled against me by my antagonist were heinous, to say the least, and were unfortunately taken seriously by many due to the smoke/fire assumption. I was publicly accused of child abuse, fraud, theft, tax evasion and many other crimes including veiled language suggesting a murder conspiracy. My accuser's anti-social personality is a matter of record with a trail of chaos, destroyed lives, destroyed careers, two gravestones, and many serious criminal and civil offenses. Notwithstanding, the allegations were taken seriously by many who were not privy to this history. In May 2009 this person was finally arrested for criminal charges in two states and spent 10 nights in a Nebraska jail as a fugitive from justice from Iowa. Criminal trials are still pending at the time of writing.

It had taken me 20+ years to build my resume and reputation. Naturally anyone considering employing, partnering or contracting with an individual in any substantial way is going to *"Google him"* (gender inclusive). The first search conducted will probably be the person's name and the name of his or her most recent business or employer. The efficiency, availability and reach of Google and other search engines has in a few short years permitted a person's enemy to turn the victim's greatest vocational asset into a liability; that asset being his or her resume or CV. In the case of an innocent victim this is a bad thing but where the allegations do have basis in fact, it is a positive development. I am sure many crimes have been averted due to the dissemination of information about convicted child molesters when they move into new communities, for example.

Closing Thought

"Do everything you can to live a quiet life. Mind your own business. Work with your hands, just as we told you to. Then others will have respect for your everyday life. And you won't have to depend on anyone." 1 Thessalonians 4:11-12

Disclaimer

This essay should not to be construed as legal, medical or mental health advice. This essay was not authored by or sponsored by an attorney, physician or therapist and is provided for informational purposes only and is not intended to express or constitute legal, medical or counseling advice to any reader. No attorney-client relationship between the reader and any attorney is created by the essay, and no reader should act or refrain from acting on the basis of any content in the essay except in reliance upon the advice of a qualified attorney licensed to practice in the reader's or other applicable jurisdiction. The author is not an attorney or a firm of attorneys and is not licensed to practice law in any jurisdiction.

8

Cyberbullying Is Worse than Offline Bullying

Gideon Lasco

Gideon Lasco is a physician, medical anthropologist, and writer working in the Philippines.

There are many kinds of bullying, from taunts on the playground to physical abuse to, yes, virtual abuse. In this opinion piece, the writer discusses the immense damage that can be done when bullies take to cyberspace. He makes the case for why cyberbullying is worse than in-person bullying—citing opportunity, reach, and anonymity. The right to free speech is important, Lasco acknowledges, but we also need to have a serious conversation about civility and do more to combat bullying.

Like many others, I experienced both being bullied and being the bully when I was a child. I remember one tumbang preso game in our neighborhood in which I was the taya (or what Americans might call the "it"). In this game, the taya must keep a large tin can standing until he manages to touch another player. What makes this a challenge is that the other players will keep hurling their slippers to fell the can - -often hitting the taya in the process. As one of the youngest kids playing the game, I managed to end my turn only after so many slipper hits, jeers and taunts.

I don't think that situation will ever happen again. And it's not just because very few kids play tumbang preso these days, but

"Cyberbullying Is Worse Than Bullying," by Gideon Lasco. March 16, 2016, Philippine Daily Inquirer. http://opinion.inquirer.net/93800/cyberbullying-is-worse-than-bullying. Reprinted by permission of the Philippine Daily Inquirer, Inquirer.net.

also because bullying has taken a different form—on top of the "traditional" bullying that still goes on in schools. Just like many games children play nowadays, bullying has moved to cyberspace, to devastating effect.

The case of Stephen Villena, the University of the Philippines Los Baños student who drew ire on social media for his seemingly disrespectful interrogation of presidential candidate Rodrigo Duterte, is illustrative. Taken out of context, his line of questioning went viral, quickly eliciting outrage from many of the Davao mayor's supporters. While others merely called out Villena for supposed lack of respect and poor choice of words, the backlash has reached a point where some are actually calling for his death, and the poor kid has reportedly received death threats.

Cyberbullying can actually be worse than bullying, and it is a moral imperative for us as a nation to seriously deal with this phenomenon as it can take a heavy toll on individuals—specially the youth—and our society.

First of all, what makes cyberbullying worse is that there is no place to hide. For kids who get bullied in school, bullying ends as soon as they've taken the ride home. But in cyberbullying, even at home, with our 24/7 Internet connectivity, victims can see hateful words as long as they are awake. You can say that they can simply deactivate their social media accounts, but in this age where the Internet means a lot of things—from communicating with friends to playing games—specially for young people, the mere act of having to deactivate one's account is part of the damage done.

Secondly, with cyberbullying, your being bullied is exposed to so many people, making the burden of it even heavier. For obvious reasons, kids are embarrassed to tell their parents that they're being bullied in school. But in cyberbullying all the insults hurled at them are exposed to all their social circles, never mind the general public. Surely, it can get too much for any person, let alone a teenager like Villena, to handle.

Finally, the nature of the Internet makes it much easier for people to say hurtful words—not just because they are protected by anonymity and distance, but because they don't get to see the emotional toll they inflict on the people they're bullying. In school, if someone is already crying and screaming, the bullies will (usually) stop the punches. The problem with the Internet, however, is not just that it has become so easy to hurt people, but that you don't even realize that you're hurting them.

By the time celebrities have become famous enough to earn a following of haters, they would have learned not to care. But we must ask ourselves about the morality of thrusting one kid's mistake into the limelight and casting stones—even death threats—on him. This is not a question of politics, but of ethics: One can support Duterte and be outraged about the backlash Villena has received. One can rebuke Villena's behavior and still protest the gross incommensurability of people's reactions. As Duterte's own campaign rightfully cautioned, we must "exercise civility, intelligence, decency and compassion when engaged in any discourse."

Free speech, whether online or offline, is enshrined in our democracy and we need to give maximum tolerance to people's ways of expressing themselves. But we need a serious conversation about how we can achieve a more civilized discourse in the Internet. One way could be to teach the ethics of social media as soon as kids start toying with iPads, mindful that cyberbullying happens in a smaller, but no less damaging, scale in schools. In this effort we need more inputs from various disciplines—from psychologists and sociologists to communications specialists and IT experts, among many others.

The media, by thrusting people into fame or notoriety, have a big share in this responsibility. I refer not just to the mass media but also to social media outfits and even individual users that can make an issue go viral and facilitate its reportage to media-at-large. We, too, can inflict emotional damage on the people we post about. As with the mass media, social media's guiding principle must not be the sensationalist drive toward more page views, likes and shares, but a commitment to truth, fairness and justice.

If it's any consolation, the nature of viral hate is such that it moves on to the next victim in a matter of days. Even so, one day of experiencing hate is one day too many. With studies showing that victims of cyberbullying are at risk for depression, school and work underperformance, health problems, and increased likelihood to commit suicide, much is at stake in this issue.

Bullies we may not be, but neither can we afford to be mere spectators.

9

Charges Fade But a Bad Reputation Is Forever

Alison McCook

Alison McCook is a science writer and editor who was deputy editor of the Scientist *when she wrote this article.*

The internet doesn't just wreak havoc on bullies, abuse survivors, and celebrities. Professional communities and scientific reputations can feel the hit as well. Here, a journalist shares the stories of three researchers who were found guilty of relatively minor acts of scientific misconduct and barred from receiving federal funds for a period of three years. However, many years later, a Google search for their names (which have been changed in the article) still turns up the details of their infractions, creating professional and often personal obstacles for these people whose names have been officially cleared.

E ach year, the U.S. Office of Research Integrity (ORI) investigates dozens of charges of scientific misconduct. And each year, the ORI adds a handful of names to a list of researchers found guilty of falsifying figures, fabricating data, or committing other academic infractions. As of April 1, 2009, this Administrative Actions list, presented on the ORI Web site, carried 38 names. These people are barred from receiving federal funds and/or serving on a Public Health Service committee, typically for a period of 3–5 years. Once the debarment term is up, the name disappears from the list. In theory, the punishment—and the shame—of the ordeal is over.

"Life After Fraud," by Alison McCook. Reprinted by permission. The original article appeared in the July 2009 issue of *The Scientist* and can be accessed online at http://www.the-scientist.com/?articles.view/articleNo/27474/title/Life-After-Fraud/.

However, any time the ORI makes a formal ruling of misconduct, that information ends up on the Internet. The ORI's newsletter and annual reports, which used to be hard copies sent to federally funded schools, are now all electronic. The NIH Guide, a weekly report that lists findings of misconduct to help grant reviewers flag scientists who apply for federal funds before their exclusion period is over, is online, too. And the Federal Register, the official publication of every federal agency, is available as a daily email digest. So Google anyone's name who has ever been penalized by the ORI, and even if their debarment was lifted more than a decade ago, even if they signed a document stating they accepted the ORI's decision well before the Internet became such a staple of daily life, the description of the finding against them—and the penalty they received—will pop up. In some cases, it's the first article that appears.

Of the hundreds who faced federal reprimands in the last 20 years, three agreed to speak to the *Scientist* about their experience. All spoke on the condition that the story would not include their real names. Doing so, of course, would only create one more unpleasant entry in what comes up when you enter their names into an online search engine.

It was the deadline of the most important decision molecular biologist Daniel Page had ever had to make in his career, and he didn't know what to do. In his hands were papers listing a series of charges of scientific misconduct against him—penalties his institution, Ohio State University, was asking him to accept. The hardest one: admitting guilt.

The charges were relatively minor. It all came down to company data Page had included in a grant application that he says he believed he had permission to use, but the company says he didn't. A couple of oversights on Page's part led to accusations of plagiarism, falsification of qualifications, and breach of confidentiality. He didn't mind having to take a class on misconduct, withdrawing his application for early tenure, and writing letters of apology to some of the people involved. But even after several months of an emotional investigation, during which he hadn't been sleeping well and his relationship with his fiancée had been deteriorating, he just wasn't sure he was willing to admit guilt to something he says wasn't true.

"So I came into work on the deadline day still not knowing what to do," Page recalls. "I turned on my computer, and a plane hit the World Trade Center. And then another plane hit the World Trade Center. And then another plane hits the Pentagon." It was the morning of September 11, 2001. When he realized the enormity of what was happening, his concerns about signing the paperwork melted away. "I realized there were a lot bigger things in the world." He signed a declaration of guilt, and handed it over to OSU officials that day. The school passed on its findings to the ORI. Eventually, the ORI added Page to its Administrative Actions list.

In 2007, the ORI received 222 allegations of misconduct, opened 14 new cases of misconduct, and closed another 28. Ten of those closed cases resulted in findings of misconduct and/or administrative actions.

Once he signed the document, Page told his department what had happened, met one-on-one with 14 faculty members with whom he had close research collaborations, and explained the situation to his graduate students. "I'd like it to go away, but I haven't tried to hide from it," he says. For the most part, people accepted his side of the story. "The people that work close to me, most of them patted me on the back and said 'we trust you.'" Others were less sympathetic. One faculty member, who works across the hall from Page, still believes he is a liar and a cheat, Page says. Page never shared his story with anyone in his family, out of embarrassment. To this day, he doesn't know if they know about it.

The story began while Page was researching a steroid hormone that appeared to improve the immune response to viral and bacterial infections. A startup company, which we'll call Vaxeen (the real company did not respond to requests for comment), approached him to see if he could provide a wet research lab to do pharmaceutical work in animals, to test the hormone's ability to boost vaccine efficacy. Page agreed, and signed a contract that guaranteed him $280,000 over 2 years in funding, with the promise of more. Page decided he wanted to do a broader project, so he began writing an NIH grant with a Vaxeen scientist (whom he declines to name). This scientist provided Page with some preliminary data from the company, which Page added to the application without attribution, since the Vaxeen scientist would be represented in the list of coauthors.

Many allegations to the ORI involve "honest differences in interpretations or judgments of data," that the agency does not consider misconduct. Similarly, the ORI does not investigate authorship or credit disputes between former collaborators, even if the complainants describe them as plagiarism.

Just days before Page planned to submit the grant, however, the Vaxeen scientist told him that the company did not want his name on the application. Page took him off the author list, but forgot to remove the company's results from the preliminary data section. "Absolutely, if I had thought of it, I would have put [that data] in the background of the grant, and attributed it to the company," he says. "Rarely a week goes by where I don't think about this."

Over time, Page pieced together what happened next. A reviewer of his grant who had also worked with Vaxeen (and declined to be named in this story) recognized the data, recused himself from the review, then likely contacted the company (the reviewer can't recall if he contacted Vaxeen or not). However the company found out, it then asked Page for a copy of his written permission to use the data. Page said he thought he had received permission from his collaborator, without needing a written agreement. "Absolutely, I was caught," he says. OSU investigated—going through his files, computer hard drive, and all communications with the company— and concluded that Page "had committed scientific misconduct under federal and university guidelines," according to a university statement issued at the time. (An OSU spokesperson declined to comment further on the case.) Page thought about leaving OSU, but his colleagues—who largely supported him and believed he didn't intend to mislead—convinced him to stay. "If it wasn't for them, I would have quit," he says. "I'd be teaching at a college."

One year after Page signed the paperwork on that fateful day, he received tenure. Since that time, he has published 35 papers and accumulated a lifetime total of more than 1,200 citations. He now receives more requests to review papers and grants than he did before the incident occurred. For him, the hardest part is meeting other researchers and asking himself: do they know? "When they hear my name, do they go, 'Oh, I know you already.' Do they have a preconceived notion about me? When I interact with people at study sections or when I interact with people at scientific meetings, do they already know who I am before I know them?"

Gerry Levick first realized the gravity of a decision he'd made 4 years earlier while being cross-examined in a 1998 trial. As a researcher in human performance and consciousness at Touro College in New York, Levick occasionally testifies as a forensic consultant in court cases—in this one, he spoke about whether he believed a driver was paying attention when a car accident occurred.

While being cross-examined, the lawyer asked him if he had ever been found guilty of scientific misconduct. He said no. Had he ever been censured by a professional organization? No. Had he ever been found guilty of misconduct by a professional organization? No again. Then came the most direct question: Had he ever been convicted of professional misconduct by the National Institutes of Health? "And then it hit me. I said, 'Oh my God.' " The attorney immediately presented official documents showing that, in 1994, Levick had agreed to be penalized for misrepresenting his qualifications and expertise on a grant application. Levick had signed a document, but had never admitted guilt, and he believed that the penalty period had expired in 1997.

The judge cleared the jury from the room, and told Levick he could not continue his testimony. Levick stepped down from the witness stand, embarrassed and perplexed. How had the lawyer found out about something that ended a year ago? "I couldn't figure out what had happened, where this came from. I didn't realize it was in the public domain." The charges stemmed from the wording Levick used on an NIH training grant application he submitted in 1988, when he was 39. He no longer has the original application, and sometimes struggles to remember exactly what he wrote. First, the agency alleges he claimed he had an MD degree from the University of Manchester—Levick admits that he wrote that on his application, but his real degree was an MBChB, a Bachelor of Medicine and Bachelor of Surgery that, in the United Kingdom, represents a combined undergraduate and graduate degree that serves as the initial step students take who want to become doctors. (Levick eventually obtained an MD from a university in Sri Lanka.) He says he wanted to simplify the process since this type of degree doesn't exist in the United States. Second, Levick said he was based at Harvard Medical School (HMS), when his real affiliation was, according to Levick, "the Child Study Unit" at Children's Hospital Boston, a teaching hospital of HMS. His funding, he says, came from the Research Foundation of Harvard University. When describing his role at Harvard, "I think I said that I was, uh, associated. I think the word was associated, or a fellow. I actually don't remember." (A Harvard Medical School spokesperson confessed that there are many groups associated with Harvard, but he had never heard of the Research Foundation.) The final charge is that he falsely claimed to have 13 patents—Levick says he wrote 13 patents "and technologies," representing new tools modeled on older inventions.

"I'm angry as hell. And there's nothing whatsoever I can do about it."

"They were looking to see if the t's were crossed, the i's were dotted. And admittedly sometimes they weren't," he says. "Maybe I wasn't careful enough, maybe I was. But the sum and substance of this stuff has no merit."

"They" in his story represents investigators at the New York Chiropractic College (NYCC), where Levick was affiliated between 1986 and 1990, then based in Long Island. As a member of the board of trustees, Levick says he was privy to heated discussions about the college's decision to move its central campus upstate (a move that ultimately took place), and he suspects that board members decided to investigate him as a way to muscle him out. The college found some discrepancies on the grant application (which was never funded) and passed its conclusions on to the ORI. Given how long ago the events took place, an NYCC spokesperson could only confirm the dates of Levick's appointment, and had no details about the investigation.

In 1994, Levick received a letter from the ORI saying he was being accused of misconduct. It rattled him. "I'm a really strong character, but I was probably nonfunctional for a couple of days. All the blood drained out of the upper portion of my body. I felt pretty helpless." He consulted an attorney, who said that fighting the case would cost $150,000. Levick was in the midst of a divorce, already $120,000 in debt to attorneys. He contacted the ORI. "They said 'well, we can make you an offer.'" If he signed a voluntary exclusion agreement, he would forego federal funds for 3 years, ending in 1997. "And I said, 'and that's the end of that?' They said 'yeah.' I did ask them whether this would appear anyplace. And they said 'no.' And I said 'okay.'"

On average, an ORI investigation takes 19 months overall to conclude. Around one-third of researchers investigated for misconduct by the ORI are eventually found guilty. Of the 10 findings of misconduct in 2007—all of which involved falsification or fabrication of data—seven scientists were barred from receiving federal funds. Two scientists were barred for 5 years; one was barred for life.

Fifteen years later, sitting in his tiny, windowless Long Island office at Touro College on one of the first sunny spring days of the year, surrounded by richly colored paintings and drawings that cover every wall, Levick catalogues the impact that decision has had on his life.

He estimates that he has applied to hundreds of institutions, none of which hired him. He says has published more than 300 academic papers, and comes with millions in funding—student tuition (he works with 13 PhD students), a $650,000 yearly contract for 12 years from the F. R. Carrick Institute, as well as grants over the years from state and federal agencies. Just this past winter, he received an offer of full professor from a university in Israel (he declined to name which one), along with money for travel and to build a lab. "I told them this story, because I wanted there to be no chance of there being a problem. They said 'we're going to investigate,' etcetera. And they did." The faculty senate cleared him, but the president of the university reneged on the offer. "I felt like shit warmed over," Levick says. "It was really painful."

Once he realized that his misconduct was on the Web for all to see, he wrote to then-head of the NIH, Elias Zerhouni, asking if he could take down the information, considering that he was "unemployable as a result." One month later, Levick received an email from a representative from the NIH's Office of the Director. It simply said:

You recently contacted Dr. Zerhouni via e-mail concerning the voluntary exclusion you signed ten years ago. Your concern relates to access to this information on the web. I assume that you refer to the citation in the [date omitted] NIH Guide for Grants and Contracts. If so, please understand that this is a publication and therefore is not subject to redacting. In addition, it is clear from the announcement that the exclusion was for a term of three years and is no longer in effect.

ORI's Response

John Dahlberg, director of the division of investigative oversight at the ORI, did not speak about any of these particular cases, but acknowledges that having an official record of misconduct is a "heavy burden." However, the ORI has no control over the NIH Guide or the Federal Register, and can't take down its annual reports when they contain notices that have expired, he says. The agency does remove the names from the Administrative Actions listing once the penalty period is up, Dahlberg notes, because that information typically comes up very quickly in an online search. Still, he adds, there is a public benefit to making misconduct findings public, and easily retrievable. For every case of misconduct the ORI catches, there are many more the agency misses, Dahlberg says, and announcing every guilty finding sends a message. "It's creating a deterrent effect. When we publicize findings of misconduct, it makes people more aware of the consequences of their actions." But to the scientists at the heart of misconduct findings who want to continue their careers, the public benefit offers little consolation, he adds. "There's collateral damage. I regret it."

If you type his full name into Google, the first article that appears is the notice of misconduct. (In part because of that, Levick now publishes mostly under "Gerry," not "Gerald.") The night he and I met in his office, Levick flew to Israel to deliver a lecture and discuss more details about another offer he just received from a "major university" there. His contract at Touro ends June 30, and he has nothing lined up. Again, that offer from the Israeli university fell through at the 11th hour—the result, Levick believes, of the public information about his voluntary exclusion agreement, which ended 12 years ago. "I'm angry as hell," he says. "And there's nothing whatsoever I can do about it."

After his wife died 3½ years ago, John Franklin, 67, started dating again. On a first date, a woman asked him about something she'd found on Google. As of this spring, if you put his (real) name into the search engine, the eighth entry is a 1990 news article about concerns that a blood test to detect cancer that Franklin developed didn't perform as he claimed. Six entries below that is the NIH Guide's entry about Franklin. It stated that he fudged data in a grant application to show that the test was more accurate, sensitive, and specific than it was. He was barred from federal funding for 3 years.

Franklin explained to the woman that he, in fact, was the person in those articles. Had he known that the details would be so permanently fixed on the Internet, however, he says he never would have signed the document accepting the ORI's ruling of misconduct. But it was the mid-1990s, before the Web became such a fixture itself.

Franklin doesn't dwell on the details of his case or replay the decisions he made. Much of it he can no longer remember, though he does recall contacting the ORI once he realized his case was so prominent and permanent. "I called up the NIH and said it's supposed to be taken down [after three years, after the penalty was up]," he says. "If they say [the record] is going to be expunged in three years, it should be," Franklin says.

The problems began for him while he was an associate professor at Harvard Medical School, working on a technology to diagnose cancer from blood plasma. He found that nuclear magnetic resonance (NMR) scans of blood lipids appeared to spot tumors before X-rays, and months or years before people showed clinical signs. Franklin published his findings in the *New England Journal of Medicine*; however, soon after, the journal published research by independent groups that were unable to confirm his results.

"I probably wouldn't have signed [the exclusion agreement] had I known it would come up on the internet 10 years later."

Franklin says that elevated levels of blood fat or improper handling or preparation of samples can influence NMR scans and lead to false results. Franklin was consistently able to make the diagnostic work, and he denies ever fudging any data along the way to improve its performance. However, a company that licensed the technology based on Franklin's initial data failed to show in its own research that the technique worked.

In the midst of all that, one Sunday in October 1993, on his way to church, Franklin began feeling chest pains. He went to the doctor and learned that his cholesterol had spiked as a result of stress, and caused an almost total occlusion of a coronary artery. "It was while I was in the hospital that the clinical trial results [from the company] came in. And they were terrible."

After the negative results, the company had to fold. It sued Franklin and Beth Israel Hospital, where Franklin was working; a sheriff came to Franklin's house on a weekend to serve him papers; and the school launched an investigation, consisting of two informal 1-hour meetings with a committee of administrators and professors.

Between 1992 and 2001, an average of 1 in 70 institutions reported investigating misconduct each year, according to a 2004 ORI report. Of these institutions, 55% reported only one suspected misconduct, 29% reported between two and five cases of suspected misconduct, and the rest reported between six and 20 cases.

Before HMS could make a ruling, Franklin left voluntarily. He had lost his funding from the company when it went under, and "I figured, with a heart attack and everything, I needed a change of life." HMS's official statement noted that the school investigated the allegations but Franklin resigned "prior to the completion of the institutional proceedings." The *NEJM* never corrected, retracted, nor issued an expression of concern about Franklin's paper.

Eventually, Franklin received a letter from the ORI saying it was conducting its own hearing about his NMR data, inviting him to attend and defend himself. Franklin says he could not bring the data with him, though, as Beth Israel was holding onto it due to the ongoing lawsuit with the company, so he didn't attend. Then, when he received a letter about the agency's concerns related to a grant application about NMR, "I wasn't surprised." Even though he says he did nothing wrong, he signed the letter, essentially accepting the agency's ruling and penalty. "I did believe then that the public record would be expunged in three years," he says. "I probably wouldn't have signed if I had known it would come up on the Internet 10 years later."

In the mid-1990s, at the age of 54, Franklin set up a new lab in his kitchen. With a hotplate, a stirrer, and funds from his retirement account, he began experimenting with new ways of delivering drugs topically through the skin. His first target was arginine, an amino acid that the body converts to nitric oxide, which boosts blood flow. (His wife always complained of cold hands.) Franklin found that if he added salt to a charged compound like arginine, the salt helped push the compound into the tissue. Tweaking the pH and changing the ratio of water and fat in the cream made things even easier. A pilot study published in *Diabetes Care* showed that the cream raised foot temperatures in 13 diabetics (who are prone to circulation problems) by several degrees, and improved blood flow.

Misconduct cases appeared to cluster in the upper echelon of institutions. Between 1992 and 2001, the top 75 institutions (ranked by NIH funding out of a pool of more than 2600) represented 29% of the institutions that investigated misconduct. Only one of the top 50 institutions did not report any possible cases of misconduct during that 10-year period.

Sitting at the head of a shiny cherry-colored table in his new office this past spring, Franklin crosses his legs and describes his life since the ORI's ruling. It's the day of the Boston Marathon, so the streets of Cambridge are unusually quiet outside the window of the small office park. Behind him hang four framed patents, all related to the new transdermal technology. His new company, which he does not want named, now makes up to $1 million each year in mail order sales of the "warming cream" and other topical deliveries of arginine. He has a list of 100 drugs he'd like to develop, funding from "rich private investors" (whom he won't disclose), is in talks with four companies to license the technology, and is at work on an investigational new drug application for topical ibuprofen to treat knee pain, which he'll submit to the FDA this summer. "I don't think I'll ever retire for real," he says.

As for the woman he confessed his story to on their first date, she eventually married him.

10

Complaint Websites Ruin Lives

CiviliNation.org

CiviliNation is an online organization that offers advice, education, and resources that promote the democratic and truthful exchange of ideas on the internet without fear of abuse or harassment.

In this 2012 interview, CiviliNation talks to Janice Duffy, who sued Google Australia after unsuccessfully trying to have damaging and untrue information removed from the search engine's results. Since this post was published, Duffy won her case against Google, but the internet giant has filed an appeal. Here, Duffy explains what happened, how cyberbullying affected her life and career, and makes a few suggestions for scrubbing misleading information from the internet.

As a result of posting on what at the time she thought was a legitimate complaint website, with other members of a support group for people at a vulnerable stage in their lives, Janice Duffy, Ph.D. became the victim of online attacks and defamation that destroyed her reputation and career. After numerous attempts over a two-year period to have the damaging and false information about her removed from the site and from Google's search index were unsuccessful, Janice decided to fight back and took the controversial step of suing Google Inc. and Google Australia in February 2011. Her case is still ongoing.

"Defamation Victim Janice Duffy, Ph.D. Says that Online Complaint Sites Can Ruin People's Lives," by Janice Duffy, Civilination.org, May 10, 2012. Reprinted by permission.

Initially a reluctant anti-cyberbullying advocate, Janice now publicly speaks out about the harm and long-term repercussions that online reputational smears can have on individuals' lives.

Janice earned her Ph.D. in the Department of Politics and The National Centre for Education and Training on Addiction at Flinders University and her Bachelor of Arts (Honours) with a double major in Politics and Sociology from Flinders University, Australia. A prolific writer and speaker, she is the author of several published conference papers, refereed/peer-reviewed publications, technical reports and monographs, research reports, chapters in edited books, evaluation reports and conference presentations, with an emphasis on public health and addiction.

CiviliNation: You have been on the receiving end of severe reputational smears and defamatory attacks, including accusations of stalking, blackmail, computer hacking and fraud. Please share your story with us.

Janice Duffy: I really appreciate the chance to share my experience with CiviliNation, but I admit there was a time when I did not want to speak about it. I actually feared my case becoming public and only started talking about it when it became clear I couldn't evade the media any longer. I suppose it's to be expected that one cannot quietly sue a company such as Google and go unnoticed. My attorney filed proceedings in February 2011 and I refused to comment publicly until November of last year. When I became aware that the media had obtained the court's permission to access the case files, and the defamation against me was still highly visible on Google, I decided to start a blog in order to share my story. I have subsequently provided comments to the media in Australia, but I contacted CiviliNation because doing so is a chance to possibly provide benefit to others on a broader and international scale. Hopefully I will be able to share news of a successful outcome to my case some time in the future.

As is typical in many other situations, I was cyberbullied by a person or persons unknown to me. I was part of an online support group that posted about scam artists taking advantage of vulnerable people on what we thought was a legitimate website, Ripoff Report. Because I wasn't aware of the actual nature of how Ripoff Report does business, I registered on the website using my real name and identifying information. I registered using my real identity because I believe it is cowardly to publish material that is critical about a person or a business on an anonymous basis. However, unbeknownst to me at the time, the website passes on the identities of people who write complaints directly to the businesses and/or individuals that they have made complaints about. Ripoff Report's owner admitted this in a disposition in the U.S. case *The Matter of Federated Financial Services, Inc. vs. Xcentric ventures, LLC, Ed Magedson, et al Case No. CACE0401772 (21) Broward County 17th Judicial District of Florida*, and the Honorable Charles R Norgle, the judge in a later case *George S. May International Company, Plaintiff, v. Xcentric Ventures, LLC, Ripoffreport.Com, Badbusinessbureau. Com, Ed Magedson, Various Abc Companies, Jane and John Does, Defendants. No. 04 C 6018. United States District Court, N.D. Illinois, Eastern Division, 2004*, accepted evidence in discovery that the site tried to sell off lists of consumers to class action attorneys for $800,000 USD.

As a result of Ripoff Report's common practice of passing along the identity of people who make reports on its website, many people like me are cyberbullied as a "revenge attack" for posting business reviews. My unlisted mobile number was published on Ripoff Report, and I know the only way my attacker(s) could have obtained it was from my login details to the website, which the site shared. Ripoff Report also published a post that urged readers to harass me, which lead to me receiving threatening phone calls. It has been a nightmare and, more than four years after the material was first published on the site, it is still ongoing.

Not surprisingly, Ripoff Report doesn't remove material even when it can be proven false or defamatory, nor even when, as in my case, a user is cyberbullied as a result of submitting a complaint. There is a recent Florida case in which the judge wrote:

The business practices of Xcentric, as presented by the evidence before this Court, are appalling. Xcentric appears to pride itself on having created a forum for defamation. No checks are in place to ensure that only reliable information is publicized. Xcentric retains no general counsel to determine whether its users are availing themselves of its services for the purpose of tortious or illegal conduct. Even when, as here, a user regrets what she has posted and takes every effort to retract it, Xcentric refuses to allow it. Moreover, Xcentric insists in its brief that its policy is never to remove a post. It will not entertain any scenario in which, despite the clear damage that a defamatory or illegal post would continue to cause so long as it remains on the website, Xcentric would remove an offending post.

There is a financial reason why the site operates this way– it can earn substantial revenue from businesses that pay to "rehabilitate" their reputation instead of simply removing this false or harmful material. Ripoff Report charges an upfront fee of between $7,500 and $20,500 plus a monthly subscription for their "Corporate Advocacy Service" (see *Asia Economic Institute et al v. Xcentric Ventures LLC et al*).

Websites such as Ripoff Report have a high page rank on Google and use this prominence to generate further revenue for the "rehabilitation" of reputations. I've summarised the business practices of Ripoff Report on my blog. Unfortunately, according to a blog post by Google's SEO expert Matt Cutts, Google takes the position that "pretty much the only removals (at least in the U.S., which is what I know about) that we do for legal reasons are if a court orders us."

Although the allegations published about me are of a serious nature, they are not uncommon on the website. Ripoff Report also publishes offensive and/or defamatory material about individuals and business owners, including extremely sick racial slurs as well as accusations against people of paedophilia and murder.

The very public nature of cyberbullying increases the personal and professional devastation because it is on view to the world. Although research on the psychological impact of cyberbullying is still in its infancy, studies have identified high rates of post traumatic stress disorder, suicide ideation and clinical depression among victims. This is compounded by the powerlessness felt by victims when attempts to get the material removed are repeatedly ignored or refused. The distress experienced by victims is evident in the comments on the Remove Rip Off Report From Google" petition.

CiviliNation: What effect have these attacks had on you professionally?

Janice Duffy: The effect on my life has been profound, and at this point I feel that my career has been destroyed. After my former employer found the defamatory material about me online, I tried to keep my job – I loved working in the field of health research and was good at it – but because both Ripoff Report and Google refused to remove the material, my work environment became so uncomfortable and pressure-filled that I felt I had no choice but to leave my position before I was let go. I resigned with a confidentiality agreement in place that prevents me from going into more details about what happened at my previous employer, but I have no doubt that the outcome of me leaving would have been different if not for the publication of the defamatory material.

I have now been unemployed for 21 months and there is no point in applying for a job while the material remains online. I am facing a long legal battle and I will have to evaluate the damage on my career when I am vindicated. I fear that the damage is irreparable. Now I spend the majority of my time doing research and gathering evidence for my legal case. While I feel that I am lucky that I live in Australia where the law offers a stronger remedy for defamation (as opposed to the U.S. in which both websites and search engines are protected by Section 230 of the Communications Decency Act), it is frustrating because, but for having to fight to clear my name, I could be spending valuable time conducting much-needed health research.

It is difficult to understand why defamatory or offensive content on a website or search engine isn't removed by the site owners. The effort required to remove it is negligible and it takes only a few keystrokes. Neither Ripoff Report nor Google remove material, but instead hide behind the U.S. Constitution's First Amendment and cite "freedom of expression" as a rationale for refusing removal requests. Yet the use of this doctrine to justify the non-removal of defamatory and/or damaging material is an aberration because, in its original form, "freedom of expression" was never intended to infringe on other fundamental rights. Interestingly, both Ripoff Report and Google claim they are not publishers of material in the legal sense yet also claim that the material they publish is protected by freedom of speech.

CiviliNation: What effect have these attacks had on you personally?

Janice Duffy: One effect of cyberbullying is that victims become reclusive because the material is on view to the whole world. My name appears at the top of a Google search couched in terms such as "ripoff," "fraud," "scams," "she hacked my computer," and "she stalked me on the computer", among others. As a result, I am wary when I meet new people, wondering if they have read these lies made about me. I was a person who in the past has always enjoyed socialising, but now spend much time alone, afraid of what others might think.

When you are the victim of cyberbullying, your are harmed in several ways. One is being the target of actual attacks, which can blindside you. The other is having to endure the hit to your self-confidence and sense of safety, both which can take a long time to rebuild.

CiviliNation: You finally decided to take legal action to help clear your name.

Janice Duffy: For almost two years, I pleaded with and notified both Ripoff Report and Google to remove the defamatory material. Both Ripoff Report and their lawyers ignored my pleas to remove the material, and Google took no action either. Interestingly, Google removed some of the damaging material from their Australian domain AFTER I filed proceedings, but a link to most of it was re-indexed on Google after I complained publicly that Google removed my blog from the search results for my name.

For me, filing a lawsuit was absolutely a last alternative. I took legal action because I just wanted to be able to work, and the defamatory information online was an impediment to finding employment in my field.

I have been criticised for only suing Google rather than Ripoff Report and other search engines as well, but the aim was always to get the defamation removed from view and more than 95% of Australian searches use Google. The other search engines have been more willing to respond to take-down notifications; Bing and Yahoo have removed the defamatory material from their Australian domains and my lawyer and I have notified them to remove it from all domains accessible in Australia.

Honestly, at the time I did not think the case would go to a trial because Google Australia resolved a similar case in 2008 in which the company removed the defamatory material after the first directions hearing and the matter was resolved. However, it appears that the plaintiffs in that particular case were the owners of a lucrative Australian business and therefore had the financial resources to go to a trial. I doubt that Google believes that an ordinary person would have the financial resources to continue litigation and perhaps in my case their legal approach is to try to make my case financially insurmountable in the early stages. Nevertheless for two reasons I was lucky, at least from a legal perspective. Firstly, according to Australian defamation laws, any person or organisation can be found liable if they contribute to the communication of defamation. Secondly, I hired experienced lawyers who are willing to go the distance with me. Even so is it a long process and my dwindling resources are up against those of a multi-billion dollar company.

CiviliNation: Do you believe that employers have any responsibility in checking the accuracy of negative information found online before using this information in making employment hiring decisions?

Janice Duffy: I absolutely believe that employers should check the accuracy of negative information, but I believe that even then it would still detrimentally affect a person's chances of obtaining a job. Unfortunately negative material can have a subliminal effect on employers' perceptions, and this is more pronounced in a tight labour market.

Employers see the high page rank of websites on search engines and automatically think the material must therefore be true. It took me many months of research to figure out the way in which both Google and Ripoff Report interact – it is all about the advertising revenue – but an employer is unlikely to have the time or motivation to investigate the truth or falsity of allegations made on websites and find it easier to just employ someone else.

On a positive note, I think people in general have become savvier about monitoring their online reputation in recent years. The Australian government runs an advertisement designed to alert younger people to the potential impact of putting material on Facebook, and a whole industry, namely search engine optimisation, has developed to assist businesses with their web presence. Nonetheless, once the material is on Google it is almost impossible to get it removed and I doubt that employers are aware of this. It is easier for them to assume it is correct or incorrectly believe the potential employee does not care because they have not succeeded in getting it removed.

CiviliNation: Do you believe that search engines, social networking and other websites have any responsibilities to help stem online attacks?

Janice Duffy: In a general sense I believe that these websites cannot monitor everything that is posted, but most of the damage could be mitigated if they removed offensive material upon notification. This would certainly stem the continuation of online attacks. Search engines and social networking sites use the excuse that it is too expensive to remove material on demand and/or that they should not be required to arbitrate about the truth or false nature of material.

But both Facebook and Google enjoy a very high profit margin and these profits are derived from advertising. Therefore, in many cases they are earning money from web pages that contain the damaging material. Ripoff Report and Google both share the advertising revenue derived from putting ads on the website, including the pages that defame me. The ability to make a decision about whether material is likely to cause harm is not rocket science and as I noted above, it only takes a few keystrokes to remove it.

Maybe these companies should use their vast financial resources to fund staff positions to act on removal requests.

CiviliNation: What is your response to people who claim that online reputational attacks against adults are rare and not something that most people need to worry about?

Janice Duffy: I think that proportionate to total Internet usage online reputational attacks are rare, but it is certainly something people need to worry about. From a personal perspective, if it happens to them their lives will be destroyed. There is often no warning that this can happen, and not all victims of cyberbullying know the perpetrators, making defending one's self even harder. In my case I simply submitted a consumer report on a website I thought was legitimate and several years later I am still fighting to clear my name.

CiviliNation: Why do you think there is a frequent lack of understanding by law enforcement and the legal system about the depth and breadth of the problem of online attacks and cyberbullying against adults?

Janice Duffy: I think the lack of understanding is due to a number of issues. Technology has grown at such a fast rate and cyberbullying is a fairly new phenomenon. It is hard to understand the impact of actions that are enacted from a distance. It is difficult for many to believe that actions that do not entail physical proximity can have such a devastating effect on victims.

I don't think either law enforcement or the legal system recognises the sheer reach of the Internet or the power that it has over every aspect of daily lives. For example, Googling a potential employee is now commonplace irrespective of whether it contravenes local laws and a report on pre-employment screening on the Internet noted that over half of applicants were not hired as a result of information found on a search engine.

Google gives Ripoff Report a high page rank, and because in Australia Google is considered to be a trustworthy company, the perception is that the material is true because it is published in a prominent position on Google – and this ends up affecting every area of one's life. In my particular situation, I received threatening phone calls because a post on Ripoff Report urged readers to harass me. The threats to kill my pets were really frightening and I actually tried to obtain assistance from the Australian Federal Police and from the American Embassy, but was told nothing could be legally done.

Some people hold the view that the victim caused the behaviour by simply using the Internet. This thesis of victim blaming as a way to account for the existence of social problems was first postulated by Ryan in 1971. This is the same archaic argument that has been used against rape and crime victims. My experiences thus far indicates that this perspective is prevalent among some members of the legal and law enforcement communities with respect to the problem of cyberbullying.

Although forensic law enforcement is a rapidly developing occupation, many traditional law enforcement officers do not have the skills to investigate these crimes and it is easier to put cyberbullying in the "too hard to deal with" basket.

CiviliNation: What role do you believe the law should play in helping reduce online attacks and adult cyberbullying?

Janice Duffy: I think that there should be laws that allow victims to sue the website, search engine, or social media company that causes harm. One excuse I've heard used by Google is that they provide their products free to users. But Google and Facebook are profitable corporations and should be regulated by the same laws that provide other consumer products, even if the victim is not directly engaged in a transaction. If I am walking through a mall and a brick falls on my head the law says I can sue the company that owns the mall. This same legal approach should apply. In Australia two recent court decisions have put responsibility onto search engines for their search results: The Full Bench of the Federal Court found that Google was responsible for the advertisements it provided on its search results (Google has lodged an appeal to the high Court) and Yahoo was found liable in a defamation case against a local man (Yahoo has not appealed this decision).

Privacy legislation in the UK and Europe is undergoing revision, and the role of search engines and social media websites to protect people is an integral aspect of proposed changes. This is a positive development. However, in the U.S. Section 230 of the Communications Decency Act is a significant impediment to legal protection from cyberbullying because even if the perpetrators of the statement are successfully sued, the damage continues if it is not removed from websites and search engines. While it may be possible to compel Google and Facebook to remove material by court order in non-U.S. nations, American websites can successfully claim protection under the CDA. In fact Ripoff Report taunts victims with this law, and U.S. courts have upheld its right to publish material that is used to cyberbully victims.

One possible approach to dealing with the issue of online defamation may be the creation of independent arbitrators that handle such matters. A couple of years ago in Australia the idea of appointing an Internet ombudsman was discussed. This stemmed from a situation where a local Aboriginal man complained to the Australian Human Rights Commission about extremely racist material published on the website Encyclopedia Dramatica. Google removed the links as a result of this complaint, but now the links are unfortunately back online. Like Ripoff Report, Encyclopedia Dramatic used a tactic of individual attacks to dissuade complaints. Unfortunately the idea of an ombudsman did not progress in Australia, but I believe a similar idea of search engines and websites agreeing to remove material has been investigated in the UK.

Most victims of cyberbullying (including myself) do not want to take legal action and would be happy to just make it "go away" more easily. The difficulty with the international nature of the Internet is finding a way to stop the harassment and establishing a program using independent arbitrators is a viable solution.

Additionally, legislation to update privacy laws in Europe and the UK in line with the new requirements of technology offers promise for victims of cyberbullying. Legislation and government proposals include a mechanism to facilitate the removal of material from search engines. Most victims simply want one action to occur – to make the cyberbullying stop and remove it from public view. The search engines have the ability to make this happen, but they choose not to use it unless forced by a court order. This fact was not lost on the British House of Lords and the House of Commons, which stated:

"Google acknowledged that it was possible to develop the technology proactively to monitor websites for such material in order that the material does not appear in the results of searches. We find their objections in principle to developing such technology totally unconvincing. Google and other search engines should take steps to ensure that their websites are not used as vehicles to breach the law and should actively develop and use such technology. We recommend that if legislation is necessary to require them to do so it should be introduced."

The recent European proposals to harmonise privacy laws across the 27 EU nations included a law termed "the right to be forgotten." This law requires search engines and websites to delete information upon a request from consumers, or risk a fine of up to two per cent of a firm's global turnover. Although ratification of this bill by the European national governments could delay its implementation, it is a really promising legislative development and has the potential to mitigate the harmful effects of cyberbullying.

11

Online Vigilantism May Increase Wrongful Convictions

Simon Chandler

Simon Chandler is a writer and journalist who contributes articles to a wide variety of political, tech, music, and literature websites.

Police departments often take advantage of social media to use citizens as unofficial police informants and gather information on suspects. While this may initially seem like a good thing, the author of this viewpoint points out that these tactics can not only lead to wrongful convictions, but also violate individual rights and turn communities into what the author calls "a soft police state." In addition, readers will find examples of how social media has compromised legal cases and led to biased criminal investigations.

The police are in your home. No, not quite literally, but almost. Just like the billion-plus people who log onto Facebook every day and the thousands of self-promoters who brag on Twitter about crimes they've committed, the cops have been flocking to social media for several years now. From the Wayne County Sheriff's Office in Ohio to the New York City Police Department, they've been setting up social media accounts, all in a bid to communicate more effectively with the public and, ostensibly, to solve cases. From the perspective of the forces involved, this strategy has worked wonders, with a litany of people incriminating themselves via boastful Facebook posts, and the public obligingly responding to closed-circuit television footage with the names of suspects.

Yet despite the noticeable benefits to police departments of harnessing social media and big-data technology to transform thousands (if not millions) of people into unofficial police informants, there are numerous demonstrated and potential downsides to this change in police operations. Not only does it open the floodgates of official police channels to the slews of misinformation often associated with the dawn of the internet, but also it threatens to stimulate a growth in misguided internet vigilantism and increase wrongful convictions. If this happens on any considerable scale, then the use of new digital technologies in policing, far from strengthening the balance of justice in the world, may only weaken it further.

One of the Biggest Crime-Fighting Tools

For some departments, the use of these technologies is already prevalent. In San Jose, California, the police recently chalked a 75 percent reduction in burglaries largely up to their systematic employment of social media and technology. According to a press release, they've begun exploiting a program that "almost immediately" posts images and surveillance video on their public portals. What's more, these media postings have apparently witnessed an emphatic public response, with tips flooding in on most cases, and with six suspects being identified for the last 10 cases they've publicized. Whether these were reliable tips and identifications wasn't disclosed by the department, but for the moment, that's neither here nor there.

Similar social media boosts to police operations have been reported elsewhere. In Midwest City, Oklahoma, the police testified to social media having a comparable effect on their performance. Chief of Police Brandon Clabes declared that videos placed on social media were "helping the department solve more crimes," and have become "one of our biggest crime fighting tools [the department has] in this day and age."

Likewise, a *USA Today* article from 2012 documented how more than 40 police departments across the United States had already turned to YouTube and other social sites, with the Philadelphia police stating that social media had helped them solve 85 cases between February 2011 and June 2012 (the date of the article's publication). A couple of years later, the International Association of Chiefs of Police announced that 95 percent of police forces in the United States use social media in one capacity or another, and that 82.3 percent of the forces polled employ such media for the purposes of pursuing criminal investigations.

In other words, social media use is now a well-established component of day-to-day policing. In fact, an indication of just how well established these practices are, and just how co-opted in the fight against crime the users of social media have become, can be glimpsed if you search Twitter accounts for "police." Here, you will see a list of almost all the major police departments and organizations in the English-speaking world: the Metropolitan Police (the UK), the Toronto Police (Canada), the Mumbai Police (India), the South African Police Service, New South Wales Police (Australia) and the Nigeria Police Force. These institutions and more are now visiting social media sites daily, tweeting about and at "wanted" persons, posting images of missing persons and sharing various public service announcements.

The "Soft" Police State

Quite apart from the practical defects and downsides to the technological turn in policing (more on these soon), there is something rather unsavory and askew as a matter of principle about enlisting social media users as honorary members of the police. Given that some 72 percent of the online US population use social media sites (and 62 percent of the *entire* adult US population use Facebook), this equates to quite a large network of dormant informers, potentially — and sometimes unwittingly — ratting on their shifty-looking neighbors.

These tactics are unsavory because they have grave implications for civil liberties. Because users of social media as a percentage of the total population are so considerable, and because social media are so ubiquitous, their incorporation into routine police operations has the sheer capacity to transform the nation into a "soft" police state, at least insofar as they and the police will enjoy near-constant access to each other. Within this hypothetical state, the police will be able to process and monitor the public's online activity without leaving their headquarters, while the public will have a very immediate and effortless means of reporting any "suspicious" behavior or "useful" information to the authorities. If such a scenario were realized, then the police would become a constant, if very discreet, presence in our lives, able to watch over us and make it easier for us to watch over ourselves.

That said, whether all 72 percent of the online US population will become part-time snitches will ultimately be a matter of how effective the police are in encouraging them to make the most of the new channels opened up by the internet, and this in turn will be a matter of police resources and policy. Still, if enough of the 72 percent are interested, and if the police continue increasing their encroachment into social media, then we may end up entering some all-too-real parody of *1984* (if the National Security Agency hasn't already brought us there).

The infiltration by the police of social media and thereby "the social domain" in the abstract already represents something of a violation of privacy, a violation of the private-social realm by the public-political. Facebook's mission, for example, states that the social media site is dedicated to "people" and their ability to "stay connected with friends and family." It says nothing about providing the authorities with a direct access line to such people, or with the means of tapping the networks and social spaces they've developed as a source of information on criminal activity (then again, it's already common knowledge that Facebook has betrayed its own self-declared mission in other respects). Even so, this is exactly what Facebook and other similar sites are doing: allowing social networks to be built so that they can be penetrated instantly by the police and their various initiatives.

Such a mass-scale opening of social groups to the presence of police is an unprecedented development, and in its wake, it may arguably spur the proliferation of social media users who consider themselves part-ordinary civilian and part-vigilante. In Australia, for example, there was the case of a concerned mother who mistakenly thought a man was taking a photo of her children in a shopping mall when in fact he was simply taking a selfie next to a picture of Darth Vader. The mother then took a photo of him, posted it on Facebook and reported him to the police, having jumped to the unfounded conclusion that he was a pedophile.

Even more alarmingly, there's the development of Facebook-based vigilante groups in countries ranging from the UK and Germany to Peru, where people are now encouraging each other to apprehend potential burglars and sexual harassers, often in increasingly violent ways.

There's even the possibility that social-media-based vigilantism is itself breeding a more generalized, offhand culture of self-policing, through which people are being shamed and chided even for more personal peccadilloes. For example, in July 2015, there was the story of the two sisters who tweeted footage of a married woman sexting another man while sitting beside her husband at a baseball game. It's probable that with the increased visibility and activity of police on social media, this kind of haphazard internet activism will only be encouraged and motivated further, resulting in a climate where a growing number of overzealous people are "policing" and harassing each other in the pursuit of likes and retweets.

Trigger-Happy Identifications and Wrongful Convictions

Aside from its potential effects on culture and wider society, there are various legal and technical issues with the increasing reliance of police agencies on social media. For one, there is the potential that, far from being reliable, the information they receive from the public is racked with inaccuracies and distortions. By opening themselves up to millions of users on Facebook and Twitter, police potentially open themselves up to a greater quantity of misinformation and speculation. Examples of such misleading noise abound when it comes to the internet and social media, as is revealed most starkly by the Boston Marathon bombing and the initial misidentification of the individuals responsible for the atrocity. There are many analogous episodes of people being wrongly labeled as murderers via social media. As a result, police need to expend extra resources to sift through an expanded mass of junk. This situation also raises the disturbing possibility that wrongful convictions may increase in parallel.

That an increase in wrongful convictions is likely is evinced by the fact that, according to the Innocence Project, 72 percent of wrongful convictions are the result of eyewitness misidentifications. As for these misidentifications, they generally occur because people are susceptible to having their opinions on who they saw and who is visible in evidential imagery influenced by intervening suggestions, such as in the well-documented 1984 rape of Jennifer Thompson, who wrongly identified an innocent man as her assailant after being shown photos of known criminals by the police. What this means is that, with the increase of social media reporting of crimes by the police and news outlets, eyewitnesses are likely to be similarly swayed by the "intervening suggestions" this reportage provides.

Such a case of victims being influenced by "intervening suggestions" happened in a trial considered by the Toronto-based Neuberger & Partners LLP, who noted that the victim's identification of her assailant in court was tainted by "her viewing [the suspect's] picture on Facebook a day or two after the robbery." The same article also notes that a judge asked that less weight be given to an uncle's identification of a young person as the perpetrator of an assault on his nephew, since this uncle had seen the suspect's Facebook profile - replete with weapon and gang iconography - before making the identification.

In these two examples, the courts involved were worried that social media may have skewed the witnesses concerned toward false-positive testimony. Just as they were worried about this, so too should we be worried that the growing use of social media may skew the police toward a similar outcome. This implies that the risk of social media doesn't simply reside in the likelihood of false identifications from the public, such as with the Australian model who was questioned by police after being identified via social media as the culprit of the 2015 Bangkok bombing. No, it also resides in how the police actively mine and search social media sites themselves, preemptively flagging up likely criminals and tarring their online social networks as potential co-conspirators.

In Fresno, California, this is tangible in how police use new software known as "Beware" to calculate the "threat score" of individuals. Depending on their "data points, including arrest reports, property records, commercial databases, deep Web searches and the [individual's] social-media postings," suspects and persons of interest are classified according to a traffic-light system (i.e. red, yellow and green), with red designating the greatest threat and green the lowest.

Such software might make things easier for the police when readying themselves for a dispatch, yet at the same time it flags up one of the more unwholesome ramifications of "social media policing." That is, given the racism already embedded in the identification of "suspects," it's highly likely that "threat scores" and social media profiling will disproportionately target Black people and other people of color. If so, the "Beware" system and the expanded social media use it represents have the potential to exacerbate the marked racial disparities that already wrack the criminal legal system.

Also, as the American Civil Liberties Union has already asserted, the Fresno police's broad-brush approach to persons of interest may result in the police arriving at a scene prepared to take some unnecessarily heavy-handed and unfair action. Even though its inner workings are a closely guarded secret, the Beware program is likely unable to distinguish between someone who posts genuinely criminal material on their social media accounts and someone who, for example, is critical of the police and their policies (e.g. Black Lives Matter). As such, its existence is one more indication of how the use of social media may actually end up lowering the quality of policing, rather than improving it.

The Loss of Innocence

As other commentators have observed, the police had been trawling through social media long before Beware, and for the most part, their use of Facebook and Twitter has been distinctly problematic. Often, they use it to piece together outlines of gangs, using the available networks of friends, followers and likes to deduce who might be criminally associated with known outlaws. The thing is, this method also lacks considerable nuance and context, as it disregards the possibility that "friending" a person who has committed a crime or "liking" a video of a crime, for instance, doesn't necessarily mean you're actually in league with that person or have perpetrated that crime. In certain high-profile cases, this kind of simplicity has led to false arrests and charges, such as with Jelani Henry, who in 2012 was charged with attempted murder after liking posts by a Harlem gang, which counted his brother as one of its members.

Henry wasn't the only person to be arrested primarily for his or her online activity. In 2012, the New York City Police Department launched Operation Crew Cut, an initiative that based itself around the monitoring of social media activity, much of it coming from Black people. Since it began, numerous raids have been conducted by the department, with the most infamous being a June 2014 maneuver in Harlem that netted 103 arrests in connection with two homicides, in the process substantiating the fear that social media policing will disproportionately prejudice people of color. In the indictments authorizing these arrests, "Facebook" appears more than 300 times, and even though many or most of the arrested individuals may have carried some degree of guilt, the example of Jelani Henry strongly insinuates that some of the 103 may have been innocent. Indeed, a City University of New York law professor said just as much on the subject, stating that the police are now using social media to "hold 50 kids accountable" for a single shooting.

These cases show that, as with asking the public to help in identifying suspects and persons of interest, using social media may ramp up the scale and speed of police investigations, but at the cost of losing subtlety and precision. However, beyond jailing the occasional innocent, there are fears that the strategy of pre-labeling individuals as "gang members" or "threats" may play a role in the courtroom as well, replacing the presumption of innocence - one of the fundamental tenets of the criminal legal system - with the presumption of guilt. This was discussed in a 2015 law paper written by researchers from the University of London in the UK, who argue that the concept of the suspect now contains a recognition of guilt. They recount a drunk-driving Twitter campaign conducted by Staffordshire Police in the UK, a campaign that publicly identified people as drunk drivers, despite the fact that these people had only been charged with (and not convicted for) driving under the influence. While it's not as public, the practice of building databases and networks of people who've been charged with crimes has a similar effect. It tags people as "not 'wholly innocent,'" smearing them in the eyes of the police before they even have the chance to appear in a court of law and clear their names.

Fighting Vigilantism With Vigilantism

The paper's authors note that the use of the technology surrounding social media may deceive the police into thinking that their inquiries are correspondingly "scientific" and "objective." Because they amass data from the likes of Facebook in a more-or-less systematic way, they may cultivate an overly confident and hubristic faith in the evidence this data provides.

Perhaps this presents one of the biggest dangers of them all: that the police will think technology automatically makes them infallible. With this misapprehension may come an increase in the kinds of errors and injustices outlined above, as well as in the inability to see the latter for what they truly are. The police may begin accepting an ever-greater quantity of spurious statements from the public, and they may begin arresting an ever-greater number of innocent people, all the while convinced that their gravitation toward social media and big data insures them against such mistakes. In some ways, the receipt of false information and the arrest of innocent people will be nothing new for them, just as the existence of vigilante subcultures and bias against people of color are also nothing new.

However, given the massive scale afforded by social media and the internet, these unfortunate phenomena may very well proliferate at increasing magnitudes, combining an increase in social media vigilantism with an increase in presumptions of guilt. Such a lethal combination would lead to a surge in wrongful arrests and convictions, ruining lives and further eroding trust in the police at the same time. Ultimately, this gloomy possibility entails that if we want to prevent such a situation from ever coming into being, we must - somewhat ironically - exercise a certain vigilantism of our own. Of course, this doesn't mean we should stop using social media altogether, only that we should stop ourselves from misusing it, from allowing it to become an instrument of subjugation rather than one of empowerment.

12

Social Media Is Ruining Politics

Nicholas Carr

Nicholas Carr is a journalist who writes about technology and culture. He is the author of "The Glass Cage: How Our Computers Are Changing Us."

This is a fascinating analysis of the role of social media in the election—written before Donald Trump won the Republican nomination and then the Electoral College to become the forty-fifth president of the United States. The author compares how politics have been changed by the Internet Age to how they were changed by the advent of radio and then, later, television. Social media's tendency to favor "emotionalism over reason" and support "superficiality rather than depth" is, in this author's viewpoint, both a threat and challenge to democracy.

O ur political discourse is shrinking to fit our smartphone screens. The latest evidence came on Monday night, when Barack Obama turned himself into the country's Instagrammer-in-Chief. While en route to Alaska to promote his climate agenda, the president took a photograph of a mountain range from a window on Air Force One and posted the shot on the popular picture-sharing network. "Hey everyone, it's Barack," the caption read. "I'll be spending the next few days touring this beautiful state and meeting with Alaskans about what's going on in their lives.

"How Social Media Is Ruining Politics," by Nicholas Carr, Politico LLC, September 2, 2015. Reprinted by permission.

Looking forward to sharing it with you." The photo quickly racked up thousands of likes.

Ever since the so-called Facebook election of 2008, Obama has been a pacesetter in using social media to connect with the public. But he has nothing on this year's field of candidates. Ted Cruz live-streams his appearances on Periscope. Marco Rubio broadcasts "Snapchat Stories" at stops along the trail. Hillary Clinton and Jeb Bush spar over student debt on Twitter. Rand Paul and Lindsey Graham produce goofy YouTube videos. Even grumpy old Bernie Sanders has attracted nearly two million likers on Facebook, leading the *New York Times* to dub him "a king of social media."

And then there's Donald Trump. If Sanders is a king, Trump is a god. A natural-born troll, adept at issuing inflammatory bulletins at opportune moments, he's the first candidate optimized for the Google News algorithm. In a typical tweet, sent out first thing Monday morning, he described Clinton aide Huma Abedin as "a major security risk" and "the wife of perv sleazebag Anthony Wiener." Exuberantly impolitic, such messages attract Trump a vast web audience—four million followers on Twitter alone—while giving reporters and pundits fresh bait to feed on. What Trump understands is that the best way to dominate the online discussion is not to inform but to provoke.

Trump's glow may fade—online celebrity has a fast-burning wick—but his ability to control the agenda this summer says a lot about the changing dynamics of political races. If traditional print and broadcast media required candidates to be nouns—stable, coherent figures—social media pushes them to be verbs, engines of activity. Authority and respect don't accumulate on social media; they have to be earned anew at each moment. You're only as relevant as your last tweet.

The more established among this year's candidates have been slow to learn this lesson. That's particularly true of Clinton and Bush, the erstwhile shoo-ins. Their Twitter tiff was an exception to their generally anodyne presence on social media. They've played it safe, burnishing their images as reliable public servants while trying to avoid any misstep that might blow up into a TV controversy. Bush's various social-media feeds come off as afterthoughts. They promote his appearances, offer kudos to his endorsers and provide links to his merchandise store. What they don't do—at least until he launched a Twitter attack on Trump yesterday—is make news. Clinton's postings have been equally bland. Her Facebook feed is a mirror image of her Twitter feed, and both aim to give followers a warm-and-fuzzy feeling about the candidate.

Clinton's predicament is a particularly painful one. She's spent years filing the burrs off her personality, only to find that rough edges are in. Back in June, her campaign issued an Official Hillary 2016 Playlist on Spotify. It was packed with upbeat, on-message tunes ("Brave," "Fighters," "Stronger," "Believer"), but it sounded like an anachronism in a campaign that's more punk than pop.

Twice before in the last hundred years a new medium has transformed elections. In the 1920s, radio disembodied candidates, reducing them to voices. It also made national campaigns far more intimate. Politicians, used to bellowing at fairgrounds and train depots, found themselves talking to families in their homes. The blustery rhetoric that stirred big, partisan crowds came off as shrill and off-putting when piped into a living room or a kitchen. Gathered around their wireless sets, the public wanted an avuncular statesman, not a firebrand. With Franklin Roosevelt, master of the soothing fireside chat, the new medium found its ideal messenger.

In the 1960s, television gave candidates their bodies back, at least in two dimensions. With its jumpy cuts and pitiless close-ups, TV placed a stress on sound bites, good teeth and an easy manner. Image became everything, as the line between politician and celebrity blurred. John Kennedy was the first successful candidate of the TV era, but it was Ronald Reagan and Bill Clinton who perfected the form. Born actors, they could project a down-home demeanor while also seeming bigger than life.

Today, with the public looking to smartphones for news and entertainment, we seem to be at the start of the third big technological makeover of modern electioneering. The presidential campaign is becoming just another social-media stream, its swift and shallow current intertwining with all the other streams that flow through people's devices. This shift is changing the way politicians communicate with voters, altering the tone and content of political speech. But it's doing more than that. It's changing what the country wants and expects from its would-be leaders.

What's important now is not so much image as personality. But, as the Trump phenomenon reveals, it's only a particular kind of personality that works—one that's big enough to grab the attention of the perpetually distracted but small enough to fit neatly into a thousand tiny media containers. It might best be described as a Snapchat personality. It bursts into focus at regular intervals without ever demanding steady concentration.

Social media favors the bitty over the meaty, the cutting over the considered. It also prizes emotionalism over reason. The more visceral the message, the more quickly it circulates and the longer it holds the darting public eye. In something of a return to the pre-radio days, the fiery populist now seems more desirable, more worthy of attention, than the cool wonk. It's the crusty Bernie and the caustic Donald that get hearted and hash-tagged, friended and followed. Is it any wonder that "Feel the Bern" has become the rallying cry of the Sanders campaign?

Emotional appeals can be good for politics. They can spur civic involvement, even among the disenfranchised and disenchanted. And they can galvanize public attention, focusing it on injustices and abuses of power. An immediate emotional connection can, at best, deepen into a sustained engagement with the political process. But there's a dark side to social media's emotionalism. Trump's popularity took off only after he demonized Mexican immigrants, playing to the public's frustrations and fears. That's the demagogue's oldest tactic, and it worked. The Trump campaign may have qualities of farce, but it also suggests that a Snapchat candidate, passionate yet hollow, could be a perfect vessel for a cult of personality.

The fact that experienced candidates like Clinton and Bush are having trouble fitting themselves into the new mold isn't unusual. Whenever a new medium upends the game, veteran politicians flounder. They go on playing by the old medium's rules. The people who listened to the 1960 Nixon-Kennedy debate on their radios were convinced Nixon had won. But the far larger television audience saw Kennedy as the clear victor. Nixon's mistake was to assume that he was still in the radio age. He believed that the audience would concentrate on what he said and wouldn't care much about how he looked. Oblivious to the camera's gaze, he had no idea that the sweat on his upper lip would drown out his words.

A similar inertia is hobbling the establishment candidates today. They continue to follow the conventions of broadcast TV. They assume that television will establish the campaign's talking points, package the race as a series of tidy stories and shape the way voters see the contestants. They may have teams of digital functionaries tending to their online messaging, but they still view social media as a complement to TV coverage, a means of reinforcing their messages and images, rather than as the campaign's driving force.

News organizations, too, tend to be slow to adapt to the arrival of a new medium. Television, with its diurnal "news cycle," gave a theatrical rhythm to campaigns. Each day was an act in a broader drama that arced from conflict to crisis to resolution. Campaigns were "narratives." They had "story lines." Social media is different. Its fragmented messages and conversations offer little in the way of plot. Its literary style is stream-of-consciousness, more William Burroughs than Jane Austen. But reporters and pundits, stuck in the TV era, keep trying to fit the bits and pieces on Twitter and Facebook into a linear tale. As a result, today's campaign reports often seem out of sync with the public's reaction to events.

Think of what happened in July when Trump kicked dirt on John McCain's reputation. "He's not a war hero," Trump said in an Iowa speech. "I like people who weren't captured." In any prior campaign, such a criticism of an American veteran who had been tortured as a prisoner of war would have constituted a major "gaffe." It would have immediately triggered a narrative of trial, penance and redemption. In this familiar plot, a trope of modern campaigns, the candidate is first pilloried, then required to make a heartfelt apology, and finally, after the sincerity of the apology is carefully weighed, granted absolution. At which point a new narrative begins.

That's the way the news media played the Trump attack. In print and on TV, the putative gaffe received saturation coverage, with the aghast press dutifully reprimanding the wayward Donald. "Will Trump's Smear of McCain Doom His Candidacy?" asked a *Newsweek* headline. But the narrative, to the media's surprise, never advanced. Far from apologizing, Trump kept attacking. The tweets piled up, the public's attention buzzed to newer things, and the story died before it even became a story. With social media, we seem to have entered a post-narrative world of campaigning. And that greatly circumscribes the power of traditional media in stage-managing races. Rather than narrating stories, anchors are reduced to reading tweets.

The Internet, we've often been told, is a force for "democratization," and what we've seen so far with the coverage of the 2016 race seems to prove the point. It's worth asking, though, what kind of democracy is being promoted. Early digital enthusiasts assumed that the web, by freeing the masses from TV news producers and other media gatekeepers, would engender a deeper national conversation. We the people would take control of the discussion. We'd go online to read position papers, seek out diverse viewpoints and engage in spirited policy debates. The body politic would get fit.

It was a pretty thought, but it reflected an idealized view both of human nature and of communication media. Even a decade ago, in the heady days of the blogosphere, there were signs that online media promoted a hyperactive mob mentality. People skimmed headlines and posts, seeking information that reinforced their biases and rejecting contrary perspectives. Information gathering was more tribalistic than pluralistic. As the authors of a 2009 study concluded, "blog authors tend to link to their ideological kindred and blog readers gravitate to blogs that reinforce their existing viewpoints." The Internet inspired "participation," but the participants ended up in "cloistered cocoons of cognitive consonance."

That probably shouldn't have been a surprise. The net reinforced the polarizing effect that broadcast media, particularly talk radio and cable news, had been having for many years. What is a surprise is that social media, for all the participation it inspires among users, is turning out to be more encompassing and controlling, more totalizing, than earlier media ever was. The social networks operated by companies like Facebook, Twitter and Google don't just regulate the messages we receive. They regulate our responses. They shape, through the design of their apps and their information-filtering regimes, the forms of our discourse.

When we go on Facebook, we see a cascade of messages determined by the company's News Feed algorithm, and we're provided with a set of prescribed ways to react to each message. We can click a Like button; we can share the message with our friends; we can add a brief comment. With the messages we see on Twitter, we're given buttons for replying, retweeting and favoriting, and any thought we express has to fit the service's tight text limits. Google News gives us a series of headlines, emphasizing the latest stories to have received a cluster of coverage, and it provides a row of buttons for sharing the headlines on Google Plus, Twitter and Facebook. All social networks impose these kinds of formal constraints, both on what we see and on how we respond. The restrictions have little to do with the public interest. They reflect the commercial interests of the companies operating the networks as well as the protocols of software programming.

Because it simplifies and speeds up communications, the formulaic quality of social media is well suited to the banter that takes place among friends. Clicking a heart symbol may be the perfect way to judge the worth of an Instagrammed selfie (or even a presidential snapshot). But when applied to political speech, the same constraints can be pernicious, inspiring superficiality rather than depth. Political discourse rarely benefits from templates and routines. It becomes most valuable when it involves careful deliberation, an attention to detail and subtle and open-ended critical thought—the kinds of things that social media tends to frustrate rather than promote.

Over the next year, as the presidential campaign careens toward its conclusion, all of us—the public, the press, and the candidates themselves—will get an education in how elections work in the age of social media. We may discover that the gates maintained by our new gatekeepers are narrower than ever.

13

Fake News Impacts the Internet More Than Real News

Craig Silverman

Craig Silverman is the founding editor of the online social news and entertainment outlet, BuzzFeed.

Fake news and the internet go hand in hand, but the 2016 US presidential election set new records for how much readers engaged with and spread fake news stories—many of them quite ludicrous. After the election, the online news outlet BuzzFeed analyzed the data and found that fake news was disseminated more widely on Facebook than real news. This illustrates that online gossip and fear-mongering hurts more than just private individuals—the fate of a nation and democracy can be influenced as well.

In the final three months of the [2016] US presidential campaign, the top-performing fake election news stories on Facebook generated more engagement than the top stories from major news outlets such as the *New York Times, Washington Post, Huffington Post*, NBC News, and others, a BuzzFeed News analysis has found.

During these critical months of the campaign, 20 top-performing false election stories from hoax sites and hyperpartisan blogs generated 8,711,000 shares, reactions, and comments on Facebook.

"This Analysis Shows How Fake Election News Stories Outperformed Real News On Facebook," by Craig Silverman, BuzzFeed, November 17, 2016. Reprinted by permission.

Within the same time period, the 20 best-performing election stories from 19 major news websites generated a total of 7,367,000 shares, reactions, and comments on Facebook. (This analysis focused on the top performing link posts for both groups of publishers, and not on total site engagement on Facebook. For details on how we identified and analyzed the content, see the bottom of this post.)

Up until those last three months of the campaign, the top election content from major outlets had easily outpaced that of fake election news on Facebook. Then, as the election drew closer, engagement for fake content on Facebook skyrocketed and surpassed that of the content from major news outlets.

Facebook Engagements, Top 20 Election Stories

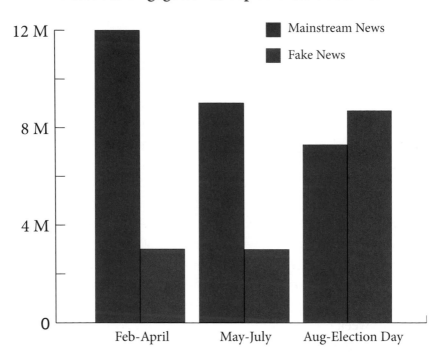

SOURCE: BuzzFeed News

"I'm troubled that Facebook is doing so little to combat fake news," said Brendan Nyhan, a professor of political science at

Dartmouth College who researches political misinformation and fact-checking. "Even if they did not swing the election, the evidence is clear that bogus stories have incredible reach on the network. Facebook should be fighting misinformation, not amplifying it."

A Facebook spokesman told BuzzFeed News that the top stories don't reflect overall engagement on the platform.

"There is a long tail of stories on Facebook," the spokesman said. "It may seem like the top stories get a lot of traction, but they represent a tiny fraction of the total."

He also said that native video, live content, and image posts from major news outlets saw significant engagement on Facebook.

Of the 20 top-performing false election stories identified in the analysis, all but three were overtly pro-Donald Trump or anti-Hillary Clinton. Two of the biggest false hits were a story claiming Clinton sold weapons to ISIS and a hoax claiming the pope endorsed Trump, which the site removed after publication of this article. The only viral false stories during the final three months that were arguably against Trump's interests were a false quote from Mike Pence about Michelle Obama, a false report that Ireland was accepting American "refugees" fleeing Trump, and a hoax claiming RuPaul said he was groped by Trump.

This new data illustrates the power of fake election news on Facebook, and comes as the social network deals with criticism that it allowed false content to run rampant during the 2016 presidential campaign. CEO Mark Zuckerberg said recently it was "a pretty crazy idea" to suggest that fake news on Facebook helped sway the election. He later published a post saying, "We have already launched work enabling our community to flag hoaxes and fake news, and there is more we can do here."

This week BuzzFeed News reported that a group of Facebook employees have formed a task force to tackle the issue, with one saying that "fake news ran wild on our platform during the entire campaign season." The *Wall Street Journal* also reported that Google would begin barring fake news websites from its AdSense advertising program. Facebook soon followed suit.

These developments follow a study by BuzzFeed News that revealed hyperpartisan Facebook pages and their websites were publishing false or misleading content at an alarming rate — and generating significant Facebook engagement in the process. The same was true for the more than 100 US politics websites BuzzFeed News found being run out of the Former Yugoslav Republic of Macedonia.

This new analysis of election content found two false election stories from Macedonian sites that made the top-10 list in terms of Facebook engagement in the final three months. *Conservative State* published a story that falsely quoted Hillary Clinton as saying, "I would like to see people like Donald Trump run for office; they're honest and can't be bought." The story generated over 481,000 engagements on Facebook. A second false story from a Macedonia site falsely claimed that Clinton was about to be indicted. It received 149,000 engagements on Facebook.

All the false news stories identified in BuzzFeed News' analysis came from either fake news websites that only publish hoaxes or from hyperpartisan websites that present themselves as publishing real news. The research turned up only one viral false election story from a hyperpartisan left-wing site. The story from *Winning Democrats* claimed Ireland was accepting anti-Trump "refugees" from the US. It received over 810,000 Facebook engagements, and was debunked by an Irish publication. (There was also one post from an LGBTQ site that used a false quote from Trump in its headline.)

The other false viral election stories from hyperpartisan sites came from right-wing publishers, according to the analysis.

One example is the remarkably successful, utterly untrustworthy site *Ending the Fed*. It was responsible for four of the top 10 false election stories identified in the analysis: Pope Francis endorsing Donald Trump, Hillary Clinton selling weapons to ISIS, Hillary Clinton being disqualified from holding federal office, and the FBI director receiving millions from the Clinton Foundation.

These four stories racked up a total of roughly 2,953,000 Facebook engagements in the three months leading up to Election Day.

Ending the Fed gained notoriety in August when Facebook promoted its story about Megyn Kelly being fired by Fox News as a top trending item. The strong engagement the site has seen on Facebook may help explain how one of its stories was featured in the Trending box.

The site, which does not publicly list an owner or editor, did not respond to a request for comment from BuzzFeed News.

Like several other hyperpartisan right-wing sites that scored big Facebook hits this election season, *Ending the Fed* is a relatively new website. The domain endingthefed.com was only registered in in March. Yet according to BuzzFeed News' analysis, its top election content received more Facebook engagement than stories from the *Washington Post* and *New York Times*. For example, the top four election stories from the *Post* generated roughly 2,774,000 Facebook engagements — nearly 180,000 fewer than *Ending the Fed*'s top four false posts.

A look at *Ending the Fed*'s traffic chart from Alexa also gives an indication of the massive growth it experienced as the election drew close:

A similar spike occurred for *Conservative State*, a site that was only registered in September. It saw a remarkable traffic spike almost instantly.

Alexa estimates that nearly 30% of *Conservative State*'s traffic comes from Facebook, with 10% coming from Google.

Along with unreliable hyperpartisan blogs, fake news sites also received a big election traffic bump in line with their Facebook success. The *Burrard Street Journal* scored nearly 380,000 Facebook engagements for a fake story about Obama saying he will not leave office if Trump is elected. It was published in September, right around the time Alexa notched a noticeable uptick in its traffic.

That site was only registered in April of this year. Its publisher disputes the idea that its content is aimed at misleading readers. "The *BS Journal* is a satire news publication and makes absolutely

Alexa's Traffic Chart During 2016 Campaign Season

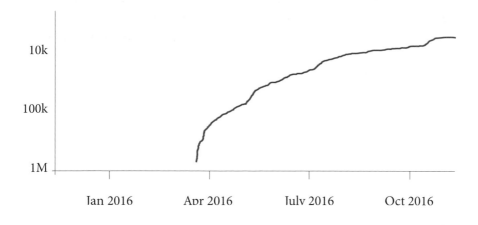

SOURCE: Alexa

no secret of that or any attempt to purposely mislead our readers," he told *BuzzFeed News*.

Large news sites also generated strong Facebook engagement for links to their election stories. But to truly find the biggest election hits from these 19 major sites, it's necessary to go back to early 2016.

The three biggest election hits for these outlets came back in February, led by a contributor post on the *Huffington Post*'s blog about Donald Trump that received 2,200,000 engagements on Facebook. The top-performing election news story on Facebook for the 19 outlets analyzed was also published that month by CBS News. It generated an impressive 1.7 million shares, engagements, and comments on Facebook. Overall, a significant number of the top-performing posts on Facebook from major outlets were opinion pieces, rather than news stories.

The biggest mainstream hit in the three months prior to the election came from the *Washington Post* and had 876,000 engagements. Yet somehow *Ending the Fed* — a site launched just months earlier with no history on Facebook and likely a very small group of people running it — managed to get more engagement for a false story during that same period.

"People know there are concerned employees who are seeing something here which they consider a big problem," a Facebook manager told *BuzzFeed News* this week. "And it doesn't feel like the people making decisions are taking the concerns seriously."

How We Gathered the Data

BuzzFeed News used the content analysis tool BuzzSumo, which enables users to search for content by keyword, URL, time range, and social share counts. *BuzzFeed News* searched in BuzzSumo using keywords such as "Hillary Clinton" and "Donald Trump," as well as combinations such as "Trump and election" or "Clinton and emails" to see the top stories about these topics according to Facebook engagement. We also searched for known viral lies such as "Soros and voting machine."

In addition, created lists of the URLs of known fake news websites, of hyperpartisan sites on the right and on the left, and of the more than 100 pro-Trump sites run from Macedonia that were previously identified in *BuzzFeed News* reporting. We then looked for the top performing content on Facebook across all of these sites to find false stories about the election.

We conducted our searches in three-month segments beginning 9 months from election day. This broke down as February to April, May to July, and August to election day.

Even with the above approaches, it's entirely possible that we missed other big hits from fake news websites and hyperpartisan blogs.

To examine the performance of election content from mainstream sites, we created a list that included the websites of the *New York Times, Washington Post,* NBC News, *USA Today,* Politico, CNN, *Wall Street Journal,* CBS News, ABC News, *New York Daily News, New York Post,* BuzzFeed, *Los Angeles Times,* NPR, the *Guardian,* Vox, *Business Insider, Huffington Post,* and

Fox News. We then searched for their top-performing election content in the same three-month segments as above.

It's important to note that Facebook engagement does not necessarily translate into traffic. This analysis was focused on how the best-performing fake news about the election compared with real news from major outlets on Facebook. It's entirely possible — and likely — that the mainstream sites received more traffic to their top-performing Facebook content than the fake news sites did. And as the Facebook spokesman noted, large news sites overall see more engagement on Facebook than fake news sites.

14

The Internet Has a Negative Influence on Americans' Opinions

Aaron Smith

Aaron Smith is associate director of research on internet and technology issues at Pew Research Center, a nonpartisan fact-center that informs the public about issues, attitudes, and trends facing America and the world.

This article analyzes data from 2011, before the 2012 presidential election, and gives an interesting snapshot of how public attitudes toward the internet changed in the five years leading up to the 2016 presidential campaign. This study found that a majority of users believe that the internet has increased the influence of extreme views, though a smaller percentage—a third—said that the internet makes it easier to counter extreme views because ordinary people have a forum for speaking up.

E ver since internet use became a notable part of political media in the late 1990s, there have been intense debates about the impact of the internet on politics. For the first time in our post-election surveys, we asked some questions to test public attitudes about the role of the internet in American political culture. The answers showed how conflicted people are about the internet: Many expressed positive views about the effect of digital technology on their personal engagement with politics, but also noted concerns

"Attitudes Towards the Internet's Impact on Politics," by Aaron Smith, Pew Research Center, March 17, 2011. Reprinted by permission.

about the ways in which the internet might be influencing the broader culture and tone of politics.

How the Internet Influences the Ability to Connect With Others Politically

When asked whether the internet has made it easier to connect with others who share their own political views, 54% of online Americans agree that it has—44% say that the internet has made this a lot easier, and an additional 10% say that it has made it a little easier. Two in five (42%) feel that the internet has not had much impact in this regard.

Demographically, Latino internet users are particularly likely to say that the internet has helped them connect with others who share their views—56% of Latino internet users say that the internet has made it "a lot easier" to do this, compared with 41% of white internet users. Those under the age of 50 are also relatively likely to view the internet as having a positive impact in this regard. Roughly half of online 18-29 year olds (54%) and 30-49 year olds (48%) say that the internet has made it a lot easier to connect with others, compared with 36% of 50-64 year olds and 23% of internet users ages 65 and up.

The one in five online adults who used social networking sites during the 2010 campaign for political purposes are especially likely to say that the internet helps them connect with others who share their views—fully 64% of these users say that the internet has made this a lot easier, compared with 21% of these users who say that the internet has had no impact in this regard.

How the Internet Influences the Prevalence of Extreme Views

Even as a majority of Americans feel that the internet has generally helped them connect with others, a similar number also believe that the internet has increased the influence of extreme views in the political debate. Just over half (55%) of internet users agree with the statement that "the internet increases the influence of those with extreme political views," while 30% said they agree with the statement that "the internet reduces the influence of those with extreme views by giving ordinary citizens a chance to be heard." One in ten online adults (12%) are not sure which of these statements best describes their own views.

Interestingly, there are relatively few differences on this question based on demographic characteristics or one's level of online political engagement. Those who feel that the internet has made it easier to meet up with others who share their views, are no less likely than those who downplay the internet's role in connecting with others to see the internet encouraging extremism. Additionally, the 21% of online adults who are active politically on social networking sites are just as likely as other internet users to say that the internet increases the influences of extreme political views.

Politically, Democrats and those who disagree with the Tea Party movement are a bit more likely to agree with the statement that the internet increases the influence of those with extreme views compared with Republican voters and Tea Party supporters.

How the Internet Influences Exposure to a Diverse Range of Views

Six in ten online adults (61%) feel that the internet exposes people to a wider range of political views than they can get in the traditional news media, while one-third (32%) feel that the political information available online is the same as the information available elsewhere.

As with the impact of the internet on meeting new people, adults under the age of 50 are significantly more likely than older internet users to say that the internet exposes people to a wider range of political views than they can get elsewhere—among internet users 67% of 18-29 year olds and 68% of 30-49 year olds say this, compared with 55% of those ages 50-64 and 38% of those 65 and older. College graduates (71% of whom say that the internet exposes people to a wider range of political views) also tend to have relatively strong views on this subject.

Those online adults who utilize the internet for political information and engagement are significantly more likely than other internet users to feel that they are being exposed to a wider range of material thanks to the internet. This is especially true for the one in five online adults who use social networking sites for political purposes—fully 74% of these "political social networkers" feel that the internet exposes people to a wider range of political views than they can find elsewhere.

Difficulties in Determining Truth From Fiction in the Online World

Americans are similarly split in their assessments of the difficulty of separating truth from falsehoods when it comes to online political information. One-third of online adults (33%) say that it is usually easy for them to tell what it true from what is false when it comes to the political information they find online, while 56% say that it is usually difficult for them to determine this. There are few demographic differences when it comes to assessing the veracity of online political information, although young adults (ages 18-29) are slightly more likely than those ages 65 and older to say that it is usually easy for them to tell what it true online from what is false.

The group we refer to as "online political users" is twice as likely as internet users who do not engage in political activities online to say that it's usually easy to tell true from false political information (39% vs. 20%). Still, it is notable that even among this relatively tech-savvy group, more than half (55%) indicate that they have trouble telling true from false political information online.

How the Internet Influences Voting Behavior

One in five online political users (22%) say that the news and information they found online in 2010 encouraged them to vote in the 2010 elections, compared with just 4% who said that this online content actually discouraged them to vote (73% said it had no impact one way or the other). These figures are nearly identical to the findings we got the last time we asked this question, in 2004 (at that point 23% of online political users said that they were encouraged to vote by the material they found online).

A slightly larger number of respondents said that the political information they saw or read online made them decide to vote for or against a particular candidate—35% of internet users who voted in 2010 said this. There are relatively few demographic differences on this question, although voters with strong views towards the Tea Party movement were particularly likely to say that online information helped them decide who to vote for. Fully 39% of internet-using voters who support the Tea Party movement and 38% of such voters who disagree with the movement said this, compared with 30% of those with no opinion of the movement one way or another, and 20% of voters who had not heard of the group.

15

Fake News and Rumors Can Sway an Election

Yochi Dreazen

Yochi Dreazen is deputy managing editor at Vox Media, a multinational digital media company based in Washington, DC, and New York.

On election day 2016, the online magazine Vox warned voters about fake news. Here, they report on the sources of some of the more egregious examples of fake news—and point out why internet fake news is arguably more harmful that misleading news reports in print or on TV. This article suggests that, for citizens trying to make informed decisions about their government, the proliferation of gossip and lies on the internet is not only irresponsible, but may in fact be a deliberate and malicious attempt to interfere with the US electoral process.

A public service announcement from your friends here at Vox: There will be an enormous amount of false information on Facebook, the internet, and TV this Election Day. Do yourself (and the country) a favor and ignore it.

Politicians have always played fast and loose with the truth, cable news networks have always gotten stories wrong, and the internet has always been a place for conspiracy theories and misleading stories and photos.

"Facebook Is Full of Fake News Stories. On Election Day, Don't Fall for Them." by Yochi Dreazen, Vox Media, November 08, 2016. Reprinted by permission.

But the 2016 campaign has seen an unprecedented increase in the sheer number of false news stories being shared on Facebook or posted to genuine-looking but entirely fake news sites run by tech-savvy young people looking to make some money off this long and bitter election.

Take the *Denver Guardian*, which earlier this month ran a story with the attention-grabbing headline "FBI AGENT SUSPECTED IN HILLARY EMAIL LEAKS FOUND DEAD IN APPARENT MURDER-SUICIDE." The article ricocheted across Facebook and gained tens of thousands of shares despite the fact that there is no such thing as the "Denver Guardian" and that the "story" in question is a complete fabrication.

It's a dynamic that deeply concerns President Barack Obama, arguably the savviest user of social media in American political history — and the politician who has been targeted in the majority of Facebook's most paranoid, conspiracy-minded, and outright racist viral posts.

"As long as it's on Facebook…people start believing it," he said during a campaign stop in Ann Arbor, Michigan, on Monday. "It creates this dust cloud of nonsense."

To make matters even dicier, many current and former US officials believe that Russia may try to deliberately spread false information on Election Day to make would-be Hillary Clinton voters stay home or simply to shake overall confidence in the American political system.

All of which means that if you see or read something on Election Day that appears too dramatic to be true, there's probably a good and simple reason: It isn't.

There's Real Money in Fake News

In November 2012, Fox News aired a video clip showing a member of the Black Panthers standing outside a polling station in Philadelphia. It was a single person at a single polling station in a heavily black, heavily Democratic area, but Fox anchors strongly suggested that it was part of a broader pattern of voter intimidation by militants determined to stop then-GOP nominee Mitt Romney. The segment was rebroadcast frequently throughout the day.

Flash-forward four years. It's certainly possible that Fox News — or a left-leaning station like MSNBC — will find a similar type of clip and present it in a way that is deliberately misleading.

Amazingly, though, that could literally be the least of our problems. A much bigger concern is the proliferation of entirely fake news sites with entirely fake stories, often operated by tech-savvy entrepreneurs living overseas.

A BuzzFeed article earlier this month found that young people in the Macedonian town of Veles (population 45,000) had created more than 140 pro-Trump news sites running posts every day that "are aggregated, or completely plagiarized, from fringe and right-wing sites in the US."

To take one example from the story, a website called ConservativeState posted an article with the headline "Hillary Clinton In 2013: 'I Would Like to See People Like Donald Trump Run for Office; They're Honest and Can't Be Bought.'"

The story was a complete fabrication, but it immediately went viral, racking up more than 480,000 shares, reactions, and comments on Facebook in less than a week. By contrast, BuzzFeed noted that the *New York Times* bombshell revealing that Trump had declared a $916 million loss on his 1995 income tax returns drew a comparatively small 175,000 Facebook interactions over an entire month.

That kind of traffic is lucrative business for the Macedonians, some of whom told BuzzFeed that they made up to $5,000 per month pushing information they knew to be untrue.

"Yes, the info in the blogs is bad, false, and misleading," one of these youngsters told BuzzFeed. "But the rationale is that 'if it gets the people to click on it and engage, then use it.'"

Trump is also getting a boost from paid trolls in Russia who pretend to be American on multiple social media accounts that they use to make pro-Trump comments on traditional publications like the *New York Times* as well as on Facebook and Twitter. The lies and false information often gets parroted by both conservative news outlets like Fox News and Trump himself.

"Are Russian trolls to blame for that?" a female troll asked comedian Samantha Bee. "Maybe people are to blame too. They're lazy and believe everything they read."

In a Close Election, a Small Lie Can Have an Enormous Impact

The bitter race between Clinton and Trump may end up being the kind of excruciatingly close race where small pockets of voters in key states ultimately decide our next president. That makes dirty tricks like recent ads wrongly telling Clinton supporters that they could vote by text all the more dangerous.

As the *Washington Post* reported, the fake ads circulated on Twitter with the exact fonts and imagery used in real Clinton campaign materials. They told Clinton backers that they could "save time" and "vote from home" by texting her name to a five-digit phone number. One English-language ad read, "Vote early. Text 'Hillary' to 59925." Another was written entirely in Spanish.

They were lies, of course. You can vote by mail or in person, but you most definitely cannot do it by texting Clinton's first name to a random phone number. It's unclear how many would-be Clinton voters fell into the trap, or who specifically was responsible for setting it. But in a race where every vote matters, the fake ads could easily have real impact.

And that's the biggest thing to keep in mind on Election Day. Facebook's enormous reach means that lies and distortions — regardless of whether they come from GOP dirty tricksters, partisan journalists, paid trolls in Russia, or money-seeking entrepreneurs in Macedonia — can genuinely impact the outcome of the campaign. Be careful with what you read, be careful with what you retweet, and be careful with what you share on Facebook. There are bad actors out there hoping to mess with our election. Don't make it easier for them.

Organizations to Contact

The editors have compiled the following list of organizations concerned with the issues debated in this book. The descriptions are derived from materials provided by the organizations. All have publications or information available for interested readers. The list was compiled on the date of publication of the present volume; the information provided here may change. Be aware that many organizations take several weeks or longer to respond to inquiries, so allow as much time as possible.

The American Civil Liberties Union
125 Broad Street, 18th Floor
New York, NY 10004
212-549-2500
website: www.aclu.org

An organization working to defend the rights and liberties guaranteed by the Constitution of the United States. The ACLU works through litigation, but also via community empowerment and congressional lobbying.

Berkman Klein Center for Internet and Society
23 Everett Street, 2nd Floor
Cambridge, MA 02138
617-495-7547
email: hello@cyber.harvard.edu
website: www.dmlp.org

A research center that attempts to explore and understand cyberspace and assess the need—or lack of need—for laws to regulate internet activity. Offers public education and mentorships.

Center for Democracy and Technology

1401 K Street, NW, Suite 200
Washington, DC 20005
202-637-9800
website: www.ctg.org

The Center for Democracy and Technology champions online civil liberties and human rights. The organization's mission is to support policies and laws that keep the Internet open, innovative, and free.

Center for Internet and Society

Stanford Law School
559 Nathan Abbott Way
Stanford, CA 94305-8610
650-723-2465
website: www.cyberlaw.stanford.edu

A public interest law, science, and technology program at Stanford University. Studies the interaction of laws and new technology to examine how the interaction between the law and technology can either harm or promote free speech, privacy, diversity, and other aspects of the common good.

International Bullying Prevention Association

PO Box 99217
Troy, MI 48099
800-929-0397
website: www.ibpaworld.org

An international organization that helps prevent bullying online and in the real world by provide ethical training and education in providing positive climates in school and the workplace.

Media in the Public Interest
2475 Broadway #205
Boulder, CO 80304
303-339-0092
email: info@mediainthepublicinterest.org
website: www.mediainthepublicinterest.org

A nonprofit that offers programs and services to help thousands of advocates nationwide communicate with greater impact, and to connect journalists to often marginalized spokespeople and broaden public understanding on critical issues.

Online Policy Group
1800 Market Street #123
San Francisco, CA 94102
email: support@onlinepolicy.org
website: www.onlinepolicy.org

A nonprofit organization dedicated to research, outreach, and action surrounding issues such as access, privacy, and digital defamation. In addition, the Online Policy Group focuses on the civil liberties and human rights of internet participants.

Yale Center for Emotional Intelligence
340 Edwards Street
PO Box 208376
New Haven, CT 06520-8376
203-432-8591
website: www.ei.yale.edu

A research organization that teaches people how to develop their emotional intelligence, and how to use emotions to create a more effective and compassionate society.

Bibliography

Books

Jeff Ashton. *Imperfect Justice: Prosecuting Casey Anthony*. New York, NY: Harper, 2011.

Jose Baez. *Presumed Guilty: Casey Anthony: The Inside Story*. Dallas, TX: BenBella Books, 2012.

Megan Boyer, et al. *Digital Media and Democracy: Tactics in Hard Times*. Cambridge, MA: MIT Press, 2008.

David R. Brake. *Sharing Our Lives Online: Risks and Exposure in Social Media*. London, UK: Palgrave MacMillan, 2014.

Matthew D. Bunker. *Justice and the Media: Reconciling Fair Trials and a Free Press*. New York, NY: Routledge, 1997.

Nina Burleigh. *The Fatal Gift of Beauty: The Trials of Amanda Knox*. New York, NY: Broadway Books, 2011.

Kendall Coffey. *Spinning the Law: Trying Cases in the Court of Public Opinion*. Amherst, New York, NY: Prometheus Books, 2010.

Robert A. Ferguson. *The Trial in American Life*. Chicago, IL: University of Chicago Press, 2007.

Tom Flanagan. *Persona Non Grata: The Death of Free Speech in the Internet Age*. New York, NY: Signal, 2014.

John Kleinig and James P. Levine. *Jury Ethics: Jury Conduct and Jury Dynamics*. New York, NY: Routlege, 2016.

Gustave Le Bon. The Crowd: *A Study of the Popular Mind*. New York, NY: Dover, 2002 (originally published 1895).

Saul Levmore and Martha Nussbaum, eds. *The Offensive Internet*. Cambridge, MA: Harvard University Press, 2010.

Justin Patchin. *Words Wound: Delete Cyberbullying and Make Kindness Go Viral*. Minneapolis, MN: Free Spirit, 2014.

Daniel J. Solve. *The Future of Reputation: Gossip, Rumor, and Privacy on the Internet*. New Haven, CT: Yale University Press, 2007.

Daniel Trottier and Christian Fuchs, eds. *Social Media, Politics, and the State: Protests, Revolutions, Riots, Crime and Policing in the Age of Facebook, Twitter and YouTube*. New York, NY: Routledge, 2015.

Periodicals and Internet Sources

Alex Bailin. "Can Jurors in the Internet Age Avoid Being in Contempt of Court?" *The Guardian*. July 5, 2011. http://www.theguardian.com.

Greg Barns. "Fair Trials at Risk in Age of Social Media." Australian Broadcasting Corporation. http://www.abc.net.au.

Jess Blumberg. "A Brief History of the Salem Witch Trials: One Town's Strange Journey From Paranoia to Pardon." *Smithsonian Magazine*, October 23, 2007. http://www.smithsonian.com.

Mark A. Cohen. "Law in the Age of Social Media." *Forbes*, November 27, 2016. http://Forbes.com.

Laura Entis. "The Crazy, Cool and Unsettling Ways the Police Are Using Social Media." *Entrepreneur*. http://www.entrepreneur.com.

Geesche Jacobsen and Stephanie Gardiner. "Legal System Faces Trial by Twitter in Age of Social Media." *The Sydney Morning Herald*, July 20, 2012.

Ariel Levy. "Trial by Twitter: After High-School Football Stars Were Accused of Rape, Online Vigilantes Demanded That Justice Be Served. Was It?" *The New Yorker*. August 5, 2013.

Adam Liptak. "Finding Untainted Jurors in the Age of the Internet." *New York Times*. February 28, 2010.

Josephine McKenna. "Italy's Court of Public Opinion Finds Amanda Knox Guilty." *USA Today*, April 30, 2013. http://usatoday.com.

Justin Moyer. "Amanda Knox Verdict Explained by Top Italian Court in Final, Final World in Epic Case." *Washington Post*, Septmeber 8, 2015. http://www.washtingtonpost.com.

Rupert Myers. "Trial by Internet." *The Guardian*. February 17, 2010. http://www.theguardian.com.

NPR. "New Details Emerge on How Police Use Social Media." October 13, 2016. http://www.npr.org.

Noah Remnick. "After a Professor Is Cleared of Sexual Harassment, Critics Fear Cultural Silence at Yale." *New York Times*, July 8, 2016.

Scott Timberg. "Why It Took So Long to Charge Bill Cosby: Social Media and Public Opinion Had to Force Hand of Justice System. *Salon*, December 30, 2015. http://www.salon.com.

University College London News. "Almost a Quarter of Jurors Confused About Rules on Internet Use During a Trial." May 15, 2013. http://www.ucl.ac.uk.

Index